Living with a Menstrual Teenager in Anxious Times

An empowering guide for mothers and caregivers

Miranda Gray

MIRANDA GRAY

ISBN-13: 979-865251-913-1

www.mirandagray.co.uk
www.optimizedwoman.com

DEDICATION

To Joanna and Amara

CONTENTS

ABOUT THE APPROACH OF THIS BOOK

'Caregivers'

There are many types of caregivers, and it would be impersonal and a little irritating for the reader if the book listed each type every time a caregiver is mentioned. So, the term 'Mother' has been used – but this does not imply that you need to be a biological mother, it simply means that you are in the role of a carer and nurturer for a teenage girl, and that there is a personal emotional bond. This also means that 'Fathers' who are looking after teenage girls may benefit from the information in this book.

'Teenagers'

Although the title says 'teenager', many girls are starting menstruation much earlier than their teenage years – so the book uses the term 'Daughter'. This does not mean that the girl involved is your biological daughter, but someone who is under your care and guidance.

This book is a guide for Mothers with Daughters of all ages as their Daughters journey into womanhood.

Caregivers with a cycle

This book takes into account Mothers who have a menstrual cycle, and it guides them through their own cycle in relationship to their Daughter's. However, if a Mother no longer experiences a menstrual cycle of their own for any reason, this book can also help them to create a more understanding and empathic relationship with their Daughter's cycle.

A book of ideas, activities and concepts

This is a book of ideas, activities and concepts – it is an enabler – and every Mother and Daughter will be unique in their cycle experiences and in their relationship. So take this information and 'run' with it. Weave the information together to create your own unique cycle. Explore, and adapt what doesn't seem to work, or create your own unique action and approach. And then perhaps share the ideas with another Mother so that she can try it with her Daughter to build greater harmony and understanding.

CHAPTER 1
WHY YOU NEED THE INFORMATION
IN THIS BOOK

It can be hard enough living with a teenager with a menstrual cycle under normal circumstances, but with worldwide insecurity, financial meltdowns, global pandemics, pending environmental catastrophe, civil unrest, increasing international isolation, and rapidly changing technology, social relations and regulations, things can be even more challenging for both Mother and Daughter to understand each other and to meet each other's needs. With two menstrual cycles living under the same roof it's not surprising that emotions run high, and that there is misinterpretation and misunderstanding. Living together in close proximity, small misunderstandings have the potential to become major disputes that affect the wellbeing of the whole family.

Many Mothers feel the need for a guide to understand the menstrual cycle of their teenage Daughters, and in that understanding to also recognise how their own cycle affects them and impacts on their Daughter. This process is not a science – there is no instruction manual for you as a Cyclic Woman or for your Daughter, instead you need to view things in the light of caring and loving exploration and discovery. If you can understand how your Daughter is feeling then you can change your approach to be more empathic and more flexible, which will not only create more positive responses from her but also allow you to meet **your needs** as well as hers **without confrontation**.

This book will help you to navigate the challenges and build a closer and more harmonious relationship and living environment.

- Understand your own cycle and your teenager's cycle better.

- Make things easier for both you and her.

- Know when and what to do, and what not to do.

- Create a flexible and adaptive cyclic relationship.

The outcome is a simple and heartfelt desire:

> To manage the complexities
> of the menstrual cycle
> in the modern environment
> with your teenager

> in the most harmonious way possible,
> meeting her needs
> as well as your own.

If you see your current situation as an opportunity to explore who you are and to observe your Daughter as she expresses herself in the world then you can deepen your relationship with your Daughter, with her cyclic femininity and with your own cyclic nature. Then you can both approach the personal and global challenges in harmony and step out into the world feeling strong and empowered and with a better understanding of who you are and what you can do together.

SHOULD I TELL MY DAUGHTER I AM READING THIS BOOK?

This depends on your current relationship with your Daughter, which phase of your cycle you are in, and which phase of her cycle she is in! Perhaps read the book yourself first to help you to discover the information contained here, and then you can not only decide if it is the right time to share it with her but also know the best way to present the insights you have gained in a way that avoids her feeling criticised or judged, or that violates her need to be alone and to shut out the world.

This book suggests throughout that you explore this information together with your Daughter and that you share experiences – and whether you do this, and how you do this, will be individual to both you and her.

The relationship between menstrual Mother and menstrual Daughter is a dance of energies. Sometimes the dancers share the same tempo and steps, and at other times they are very different. But there is always a merging of energies, and within the weaving of melodies there is a rhythm that is the same. And within this rhythm is an echo that resonates in the heart, mind and womb of the Mother – of knowing how she feels when she also experiences the same music in the same phase of her cycle.

Within the Mother, deep in her womb and body memory, is the celebration of years of cycles, of changing energies expressed and danced and creatively woven together into a life experience. This is the key to dancing with your Daughter's cycle, whether you are in alignment in your cycles or whether the timing of your phases is very different. The joy is to share this womb wisdom with your Daughter – but maybe small steps are needed, maybe you need to be more secure in the understanding of your own cyclic nature before you can understand hers. Maybe you need to read this book first and put into practice what you learn, so that you can then read it again together and discover more secrets and pleasure in both of your cycles.

The approach of the gardener

You can think of the role of a Mother as being like that of a gardener.

Imagine a rose garden full of beautiful rosebushes,

bursting with flowers. Some flowers are white, some are a rich red or a magenta pink. There are also vibrant orange and golden roses, and small pale pink buds. Each rosebush represents a woman's femininity.

In the garden there is a small clearing in which lies a smaller bush. Your Daughter's cyclic femininity is like a rosebush; as she moves through adolescence she is growing deeper roots into the earth, and her branches reach higher towards the sun. But as the rose develops it needs to grow in harmony with the seasons – otherwise the growth is stressed.

You don't force a rosebush to flower in the winter, because if you do there are no bees to fertilise the flowers to create fruits for the future. As a gardener you work alongside the seasons, helping the bush to grow healthy leaves in the spring, strong thorns to protect itself, and bright and beautiful flowers in the summer that fill the air with perfume. You sweep away the old leaves as they fall in the autumn, cut away the old stems that have died, and let the rosebush sleep warm and safe in the snows of winter.

As a gardener you are there to hold a safe space for the rosebush to grow. Perhaps you add a stake to help support it through the storms, perhaps you gently encourage growth in a particular direction, but you don't force it to grow outside of the seasons. The rosebush needs to be free to express the seasons of the Earth through the beauty of its unique self. As a gardener you need patience and time, you need to allow things to flow in their own way without forcing them, and you need to look forward to the green buds of new life, even in the cold darkness of winter.

Perhaps when you were young and having your first cycles you did not have a gardener to support you as you explored the seasons of your phases and learned the gifts of beauty, power and creativity that lie in those seasons. Perhaps you have struggled to find your own rhythm in the busy and demanding modern world. There are two rosebushes in this garden – there is your Daughter's, and there is your own.

The approach you bring to the current challenges will change depending on which phase of your own cycle you are currently experiencing. But if you decide to approach the rapidly changing social and global environments with a spirit of curiosity and adventure, of love and caring, of creative freedom, and of intuition and inner knowing, then the highs and the lows can bring you and your Daughter closer together in understanding and in love, and show you the profound gifts that lie within you both. Something incredibly good can come out of this challenging and demanding situation. And even if the change you see is very small and you know that it will take time for it to grow, there is always hope and wonder in the first buds of spring.

You can't control your relationship with your teenager; there are no rules or perfect solutions, but there are guidelines based on the experiences many women have of their own cyclic nature. And the simplest approach is to:

1. **Try something.**
2. **Observe** the outcome – 'good', 'neutral', or 'could

be better'.

3. **Accept** that sometimes you are going to get it wrong – this is not failure, just the wrong approach for a particular phase.

4. **Change and adapt** and try again.

5. **If it works, remember to do it next time.**

To flow with your cyclic Daughter, the approach needs to be one of win-win – to meet her cyclic needs as well as your own. Instead of clashing with each other or imposing your current view on her, remember that this needs to be an approach where you find a way to balance and flow alongside each other to the music. Then you will not need to force her to do anything – instead,

- ✓ she will do things for you because she feels happy and fulfilled doing them
- ✓ she will feel more open and loving because you are validating her and helping to meet her needs
- ✓ she will say 'yes' more often because you are asking in the right way at the right time.
- ✓ AND you will look 'good' and be able to get things right for a change! Her needs will be met, and your needs will be met.

The basics every woman should know

Imagine that in front of you stand four women:

> One is young, pretty, intelligent, logical, a risk-taker, independent, wanting to see the world; she needs to grow and to achieve success.

> One is slightly older, a caring mother, more emotional, social, nurturing and patient with a practical creativity.

> One is middle-aged, beautiful with a mature style, she is experienced, uninhibited, direct, intuitive, unpredictable, creative and a challenge.

> One is old and slow, beautiful in herself, spiritual, accepting, wise, intuitive and meditative.

Now imagine that these women shapeshift, and that they all look like you.

Now imagine that four girls – young women – stand in front of you.

> One girl is dynamic and intelligent. She has spring flowers in her hair and wears a short tunic. She is keen to become independent, to explore her abilities and limits, to take on the world to grow and to achieve great things.

One girl is softer and gentler. She has summer flowers in a garland around her neck, and in her arms she carries a young animal. She is caring, empathic, keen to look after others and to create a better world through her practical creative energies.

One girl wears black clothes and Goth makeup. Autumn leaves swirl around her, and she is wild and unpredictable. She is a poet, an artist, driven by highs and lows of physical and emotional energy, and creativity.

One girl sits rather than stands with the others. She wraps a dark blanket decorated with winter snowflakes around her like a protective cloak. She is quiet and withdrawn, slow to respond and rests in a dreamy state of mind.

Now imagine that these four girls shapeshift, and they all look like your Daughter.

Within your relationship are not two women – one young and one adult – but instead there are at least eight! Mothers get things wrong when they think that they are one woman – and that their Daughter is just one young woman!

What you have not been told

Most women have been raised to think that they are just one woman – linear, with a single and continuous set of abilities and physical energies. But in fact they are cyclic, embodying at least four different women – each with their own energies, dominant way of thinking, abilities and skills, communication approach, and sexual and creative energies. It is no wonder that everyone gets confused!

Your Daughter is not just one girl who is the same all the time – she is four young women expressing themselves through her cyclic nature.

If you understand how you and your Daughter experience the changes of the menstrual cycle, then you can identify which of the four women **you** are currently expressing and which of the four girls **your Daughter** is expressing. This becomes the basis on which you can build a more harmonious interactive relationship and more positive and enthusiastic communication, and it also creates the mutual understanding on which to survive living together!

Warning:

Remember this is not an instruction manual on your Daughter's menstrual cycle.

Everyone is individual in their experiences of the phases of their cycles, but there are many things which women have in common. This is a book of concepts, ideas and actions for you to explore. There is no 'one size fits all' – not for you or for your Daughter!

Being a menstrual woman is a path of amazing joy and

opportunity, of creative, spiritual and sexual energies. It is a path that changes as you experience different things in life, so no single cycle is the same, no phase is exactly the same as the previous month because each month you are experiencing the phase in a new and different situation. You are walking a **spiralling** path full of the excitement of growth and new experiences.

Your Daughter is also walking this path, and she will experience things that are similar between the months, and things that are different. But in each situation, she will interact with the world from whichever of the four young women she is currently expressing. Her world is changing fast as she is growing into adulthood, so she will be experiencing many changes in her life and more new situations in which to express her different energies. And in this time of world change, it is almost as if adults are stepping back into a teenage world, because things are happening so fast that they too are experiencing a different environment from one month to the next, even one phase to the next. Perhaps this challenging world situation can help us to understand a little better the sometimes-overwhelming experiences and insecurity that major changes can cause in teenage girls.

It's important to remember that you are living with a cyclic young woman and that you are also a Cyclic Woman. It's so easy to forget this, because the everyday world doesn't permit or reflect back this nature to remind you of who you are. It's obvious when you think about it – you have a menstrual 'cycle', and the clue is in the name. You change in a way that is cyclic and repeating. You may understand that your body changes because of the cycle of hormones, but what most women tend not to notice is that other things change as well – the way they think, their emotions, their motivation, skills and sexual and creative energies.

The section below explores the cycles that lie within the menstrual cycle – because this is **key to living in harmony with yourself AND with your Daughter**.

ANOTHER WARNING!

Never tell your Daughter what menstrual cycle phase she is in, even if you think you know.

No-one likes to feel that they are being pigeonholed or manipulated. And no-one likes to have their individual experiences dismissed.

And never tell her that she is behaving pre-menstrually – think about how you would feel in this situation! Now you know why.

You have a unique perspective when interacting with your cyclic Daughter. You know from personal experience what each of the phases of the cycle feels like. Yes, there are obviously differences – but what you have is empathy for the changes that occur and the impact of these changes, especially when the world does not recognise those changes and expects you to be the same all the time

You can empathise with the phases that bring low physical energy or energy highs; you don't have to imagine this, because you also experience it every month. Unlike the men in your family who can only imagine what it must be like to be cyclic, you have inner knowledge which you can use to support your Daughter through crisis and through life.

Please don't underestimate the importance of your experiences of your own cycle as a way to not only bring empathy and support to your Daughter but also to help her to learn about herself – and for you to also learn **from her**. She may surprise you in her observations and insight into her cycle and yours. She may surprise you in how she applies this knowledge in her life, and you can benefit from following her lead. And she may surprise you at how she supports your relationship through difficult times.

CHAPTER 2
THE ULTIMATE KEY TO A HAPPY CYCLIC DAUGHTER AND A HAPPY YOU!

Think about how you interact with your Daughter. Do your approaches, communications and activities with her take account of one or more of the following?

Her current levels of physical energy?	Yes	No	No idea!
Her current dominant thinking?	Yes	No	No idea!
Her current enhanced abilities and skills?	Yes	No	No idea!
Her current needs?	Yes	No	No idea!

If you answered 'Yes' to one or more of the above – this is wonderful, because you are already observing your Daughter and adapting your relationship to her individual cycle experiences – whether you are aware of her cycle or not. Great! You will probably have a positive day with your Daughter.

If you answer 'No' or 'No idea!' to all of the above – you probably need a little extra help if you are going to manage living with your Daughter and creating a mutually supportive experience.

A GUIDE TO WOMEN – CYCLES WITHIN CYCLES

The presence of different cycles within the menstrual cycle is something that all women should know and that we really should be teaching our girls at school. Many young women only have a basic understanding of the menstrual cycle, and there can be a reluctance to talk to their Mothers about their experiences. Unfortunately women have been taught – and it is reinforced by society – that women are the same all the time, and Mothers can project this belief onto their Daughter through their own expectation of how she should be and how she should behave.

Sadly, Mothers and Daughters haven't been told that the menstrual cycle affects more than just women's biological baby-making system – and that it also impacts on almost every area of their emotional, physical, spiritual and sexual makeup and on their overall sense of wellbeing. This book will help you to understand yourself and your Daughter as Cyclic Women – what it means for you personally in the way you perceive and interact with the world. It can also help you to see how you and your Daughter's changing perspectives can be woven together to create harmony and mutual understanding – and hopefully a deepening of respect that will evolve into a future adult relationship.

And the benefits of this understanding?

- To live in balance with your Daughter.

- To support her and allow her to support you.

- To work with the positive aspects of each phase of her cycle.

- To avoid misunderstanding and potential conflict through a mismatch of expectations.

- To live together side-by-side in the best way possible.

- To create feelings of mutual fulfilment.

And to grow in love and respect for the amazing women that you both are.

Who is with you – and when

Although this book is not about biology, you need to start with a little biological explanation as a basis for discovering your cyclic nature and that of your Daughter.

The concepts and ideas presented here are less about hormones and more about how you **experience** your cycles and how your energies, abilities and needs are affected.

Women's menstrual cycles can be divided into four physical 'phases'. Let's start with the easiest to recognise:

Menstrual phase – or 'period'

Menstruation is the time when a woman's body releases the lining of her womb.

Pre-ovulation phase

Pre-ovulation occurs after menstruation, when the eggs in the ovaries begin to ripen due to various hormonal changes.

Ovulation phase

Ovulation is when an egg is released from an ovary.

Pre-menstrual phase

If the egg is not fertilised, then the body's hormone levels decrease, leading to the release of the womb lining at menstruation.

Whether you or your Daughter are aware of it or not, each phase has an influence on your physical energies, and on your thinking and feelings. This means that you and your Daughter are slightly different women in each phase.

> You don't just have
> one Daughter living with you
> – you have FOUR!
> Your Daughter doesn't just have
> one Mother living with her
> – she has FOUR!

To help you to identify and understand each of these four amazing women, it's helpful to give them names or titles. You can create your own labels, create them with your Daughter, or use the ones suggested below:

The Four Cycle-Women within you!	
Pre-ovulation phase	**'The Dynamic Woman'** – after menstruation you can experience increasing levels of physical and mental energy and feel more active on all levels.
Ovulation phase	**'The Loving Woman'** – you can feel more emotional strength, understand emotions better, and be more caring and more altruistic.
Pre-menstrual phase	**'The Wild Woman'** – with your changeable energies you can be more unpredictable, more direct and dominating and more inspired.
Menstrual phase	**'The Wise Woman'** – during your menstruation you can be slower physically and mentally, but be more intuitive and spiritual and more insightful.

The Four Cycle-Girls* within your Daughter!	
Pre-ovulation phase	**'The Spring Girl*'** – after menstruation she can experience increasing levels of physical and mental energy and be a whirlwind of activity.
Ovulation phase	**'The Summer Girl*'** – she can be emotionally aware, emotionally mature, and caring of others.
Pre-menstrual phase	**'The Autumn Girl*'** – as her physical energies decline she can become more unpredictable, more reactive, less secure, but more creative.
Menstrual phase	**'The Winter Girl*'**– during menstruation she can be slower physically and mentally, she can lack motivation but feel more intuitive.

*Depending on the age of your Daughter you may want to use the title 'Spring Girl' or 'Spring Woman', 'Summer Girl' or 'Summer Woman' etc. Use the term that your Daughter feels she can identify with. She may feel that she is a 'young woman', where you may feel that she is still a 'girl'!

These images and titles are a very useful map for beginning to understand and identify your own cyclic nature and your Daughter's cyclic nature – a map that can guide you through the challenges of the current situation and of life in general in a more empowering and positive way.

The four Cycle-Women who live within you.

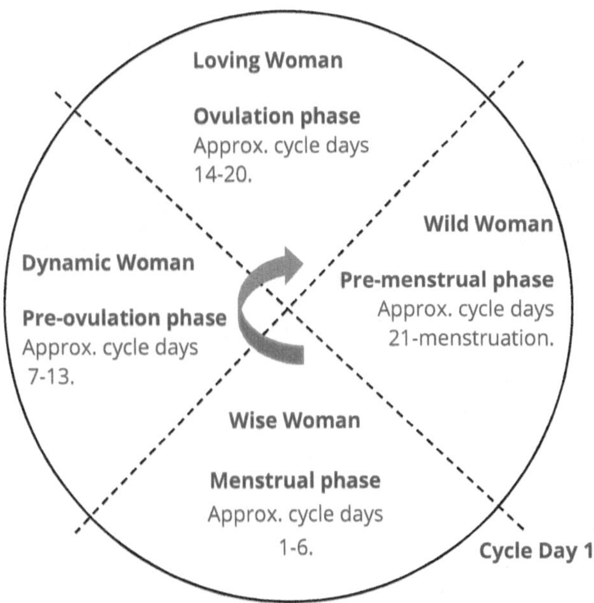

This is a concept diagram only – most women's cycles do not look like this. For example, the **average** natural cycle is 28 days – which means that there are many natural cycles that are longer or shorter. Phases within the cycle are not always of equal length – perhaps you discovered your own individual phase lengths when you were trying to get pregnant and mapping your fertility.

In real life the diagonal lines are not hard boundaries, they are simply included in the diagram to help you to compare phase to phase. Our experiences of the cycle can be more of a gradual shift from one phase to the next. So

Cyclic Women are like the moon – they change a little bit every day, and it can be hard to see the differences. But if you compare your experiences and those of your Daughter one week to the next week, it's much easier to see the changes.

It's important to know that you can also experience 'Transition Days' – days that lie between the phases where you may have a blend of experiences from both phases at the same time. So, your four Cycle-Women, could actually be eight women or more!

If you have a fairly regular cycle, you may be able to predict what type of experiences you will have in certain weeks in the months ahead. If you have an irregular cycle, then it's harder to predict what you will be like and so you have to pay more attention to what you are actually feeling and experiencing on any single day.

The four Cycle-Girls who live within your Daughter.

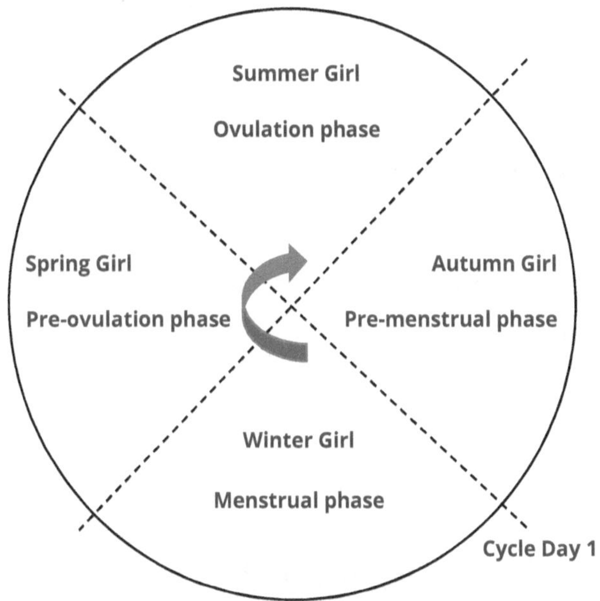

There are deliberately no cycle days placed on the diagram. This is because during the first years of adolescence menstrual cycles can be very irregular. So to build a positive relationship with your Daughter in this uncertain and stressful world you are going to need to be an observer of her behaviour to help you to understand who she is in any moment, to know how to approach her in a way that creates harmony and an enthusiastic response, and to help her to manage in any crisis.

Within your menstrual cycle are four underlying cycles that are linked to different levels of experience, and these cycles are the key to not only understanding your own cyclic nature but also to understanding your cyclic Daughter, and how to bring these two cyclic natures together in harmony.

These underlying cycles are:

- the physical cycle
- the thinking cycle
- the abilities and skills cycle
- the needs cycle.

THE PHYSICAL CYCLE

How understanding the physical cycle can help create harmony

Summary of potential physical energies

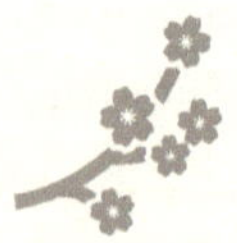

Spring Girl
Pre-ovulation phase
Physical energies:
Increasing physical energy and stamina.
Requiring less sleep.
Desire to be physically active.

Summer Girl
Ovulation phase
Physical energies:
Stable and good levels of physical energy.
Stable and good levels of physical stamina.
Receptive and dynamic.

Autumn Girl
Pre-menstrual phase
Physical energies:
In general decreasing physical energy and
stamina.
Requiring more rest and sleep.
Peaks and troughs in physical energy, with
troughs increasing in length closer to
menstruation.
Peaks in energy: physically active – sometimes
super-active.
Lows in energy: needing sleep, less active.

Winter Girl
Menstrual phase
Physical energies:
Stable but low levels of physical energy.
Stable but low levels of physical stamina.
Requiring more rest and sleep.
No desire to be active and very slow.

Women are very good at hiding their low or reducing levels of physical energy. Society expects the same level of physical energy and stamina all the time, so women 'push-through', overriding their body's need to rest more and re-cuperate. They try to show the world that they have the same energy all the time to protect themselves from being targeted as less able or unreliable. This overriding comes at a price – their physical, mental and emotional wellbeing.

The pre-menstrual and menstrual phases need extra sleep. You know what it's like when you are sleep-deprived – the next day you are more frustrated, intolerant, impatient and aggressive. If your Daughter doesn't get enough rest in her pre-menstrual and menstrual phases, then she may act in the same way. And remember that your Daughter's body is growing at the same time, so the energy requirement is huge. To help her to meet her body's extra rest needs during these phases encourage her to have cat-naps, and where possible to stay in bed a little longer.

And of course, don't forget your own cycle's physical needs too. You also need to create time to put your feet up, have a 10-minute catnap, or go to bed a little earlier. If Mother and Daughter are both pre-menstrual without enough sleep… you can imagine the situation!

The more you push any woman against her natural need to rest and sleep more in her pre-menstrual and menstrual phases, the more she will become annoyed and frustrated, and the more she will **fight back**. And if your Daughter does not understand her own need for rest in her low energy phases and tries to keep going with 'normal' expectations, then she may feel frustrated due to her inability to meet these non-cyclic expectations.

The decline in physical energy in the pre-menstrual phase is not a smooth decreasing line downwards. Within this decrease there are peaks and troughs of physical energy. At the start of the pre-menstrual phase a physical energy peak can be high and last most of the day, but by the end of the phase the physical energy troughs can be deep and long with the peaks small and only lasting a few minutes. You will know when you or your Daughter have entered your menstrual phase energies because you no longer experience any peaks in physical energy.

Note:

You and your Daughter can experience pre-menstrual energies for a few days after you have started menstruation.

You and your Daughter can experience menstrual phase levels of physical energy in the few days before menstruation actually takes place.

Remember this is a guide and not an instruction manual!

How understanding your Daughter's physical cycle can help

- Understanding your Daughter's physical cycle will help you to know her current levels of physical energy and stamina so that you can avoid unrealistic expectations about what she can manage easily – which will **avoid conflict and misunderstanding**.

- Understanding when to help and when to give her the trust to manage on her own can help to reduce her feelings of frustration and confinement.

- Understanding and empathising about why, in her pre-menstrual phase, she may feel frustrated with any physical limitations or constraints on her personal freedom enables you to help her to manage her feelings at this time, and to direct any fear and frustration **away from you**.

- Understanding that she has lower energies in her pre-menstrual and menstrual phases means that **you** do not have unrealistic or unattainable expectations for her in these phases.

- Understanding that she has good physical energy and confidence in her pre-ovulation and ovulation phases means that you do not 'take over' and shows that you believe in her ability to do things herself.

- Understanding how her cycle affects her physical energies and stamina helps you to propose exercise activities which are in harmony with her levels of physical energy and so are more likely to receive a positive response.

- Understanding your Daughter's physical cycle and sharing this knowledge with her helps her to know why she finds some physical activities more difficult in certain phases. It also helps her to reduce her expectation of having the same physical achievement level all the time-and to **play to her current strengths**.

Understanding your own cycle of physical energies also has benefits

- Knowing when you need more rest, and taking it, avoids being impatient and over-reacting to situations.

- Knowing when you have high physical energy and she has low energy helps you to not over-dominate to 'motivate' your Daughter into action, but rather enables you to find a middle path that meets both levels of physical energy.

- Knowing that you also have highs and lows of physical energy means that you can adapt your workload to give yourself a little more rest and so be more balanced in your approach to your Daughter and other family members.

As well as cyclic physical changes, you may also experience changes in your perception, emotional understanding, your natural skills and abilities, and in your motivation, creativity and needs. So to understand yourself and your Daughter better you also need to know the next cycle within the menstrual cycle…

THE THINKING CYCLE

How understanding the thinking cycle can help create harmony

Summary of potential thinking dominance

Spring Girl
Pre-ovulation phase
Thinking dominance: The Thinking Mind

Keys: Mental clarity, structured thinking
Good levels of memory, concentration and mental stamina, better logical thinking and rational processing, organised structural thinking. Impatient for results.

Summer Girl
Ovulation phase
Thinking dominance: The Feeling Mind

Keys: Emotional, flexible and adaptive thinking
More empathic, more able to read people's emotions, better communication and listening skills, positive thinking, more emotional stability and maturity.

Autumn Girl
Pre-menstrual phase
Thinking dominance: The Subconscious Mind

Keys: Highly creative, connective, inspired, impulsive and intuitive thinking

High energy moments: Highly creative, impulsive and connective thinking, compulsive thinking. Critical and looks for negatives.
Low energy moments: Low concentration, slow thinking.

Winter Girl
Menstrual phase
Thinking dominance: The Deep Mind

Keys: Connective thinking, intuitive, insightful, inner knowing
Low levels of concentration and memory recall, slow thinking, dreamy, 'whatever', more accepting or disinterested.

Men often say that women keep changing their minds. Well, it's true – **women do change their minds!**

The **dominant way** in which women think changes with the cycle phase. This doesn't mean that you can't think in any other way, it simply means that one method of thinking can be much **easier and quicker!**

But why does Mother Nature do this? She gives women four distinct outlooks on the world – so for every problem, every solution, every situation, every project, every goal, every desire and every relationship, you can view them from four very different perspectives. When properly understood and used productively, this ability has a tremendous power for achievement and fulfilment (see my book *'The Optimized Woman'*).

So, this means that your Daughter has four different

ways of thinking and of perceiving the world. It means that from one phase to the next she will be processing the information around her in different ways:

Spring Girl – perhaps asks 'why?', researching online for information, finding out what the family should be doing in a crisis.

Summer Girl – may process her feelings about the current environment and those of the people around her. Perhaps she is listening online to people's stories and sadness, perhaps she is posting uplifting messages to friends or calling family members to check on how they are.

Autumn Girl – could be super-critical of any family members not obeying societal rules and regulations and may be processing fear and anxiety about potential global or personal crises, sickness or disasters.

Winter Girl – may withdraw and not want to hear the news or people's feelings and views. She way wish to be alone to process her feelings at a very deep level.

You also have four different ways of processing a crisis:

Dynamic Woman – perhaps reacting to things logically, making action plans and organising the family to keep it safe and financially secure.

Loving Woman – may be feeling a strong urge to help in practical ways, e.g. doing shopping for neighbours, and perhaps feeling the need to make a broader positive difference to other people's lives.

Wild Woman – processing could focus on the risks to your family, being the 'health and safety' police in your home, and the fears about lack and loss. You may also be very sensitive to the grief and pain of others.

Wise Woman – may focus on processing the simplicity of everyday life, of gratitude for being with your Daughter and family, of taking one day at a time.

If there is a difficult event that needs processing, you have the opportunity to journey with your Daughter through her cycle. You can help her to see the situation from each of the four perspectives and show her how each perception is valid and helps her to create greater under-standing – but also how they help her to let go of her anxieties and fears.

You also have an amazing potential resource living with you who can support **you**. Depending on the age and maturity of your Daughter, you can engage her four ways of thinking to help you:

- Want to start some something new? – ask Spring Girl for ideas and help.

- Want help to communicate something? – ask Summer Girl for help with empathising with the receiver and with creating the most appropriate approach.

- Want to know all the dangers and risks? – ask Autumn Girl for what could go wrong.

- Want help to accept things as they are? – spend time with Winter Girl.

How understanding your Daughter's thinking cycle can help

- You can adapt what you say so your communication with her is better – appearing understanding and empathic and not confrontational or dismissive.

- You can ask her for things in a way that will generate a positive response.

- You can help her to do activities that will make her feel happy and fulfilled.

- You can help her to notice how her dominant thinking affects her schoolwork, and to create positive strategies.

- You can ask for her feelings and thoughts in a way that will open communication rather than shut the door.

Understanding your own cycle of dominant thinking also has benefits

- Knowing when you are not as empathic means you can make more of an effort to listen and validate. *(Dynamic Woman)*

- Knowing when your logical and structured thinking can appear unloving enables you to make sure that you are validating and supportive in your communication. *(Dynamic Woman)*

- Knowing when you are overly protective – interpreting danger everywhere – helps you to adjust impulsive restrictions and not appear as an irrational dictator. *(Wild Woman)*

- Knowing when you are being super-critical means you can deliberately soften your words and approach. *(Wild Woman)*

- Knowing when you want analytical discussion or an argument means you can leave sensitive topics for another phase. *(Dynamic Woman / Wild Woman)*

- Knowing when you can let go, forgive and forget, empowers you to move through confrontation. *(Wise Woman)*

- Knowing the best time and environment for you to hold a family conference, or an intervention, helps you to make everyone feel validated and loved. *(Loving Woman)*

You now know two of the cycles within the menstrual cycle. There are two more important cycles: abilities and skills, and needs and motivation.

THE ABILITIES AND SKILLS CYCLE

How understanding the abilities and skills cycle can help create harmony

Summary of potential abilities and skills

Spring Girl
Pre-ovulation phase
Enhanced abilities and skills:
- More logical and organised.
- Interested in making plans.
- Self-reliant, assertive, and self-motivated.
- Wants to achieve her goals and dreams.
- Has better levels of concentration.
- Takes more independent action.
- Likes starting new projects.
- Wants to find out more – curious.

Summer Girl
Ovulation phase
Enhanced abilities and skills:
- Wants to create new friendships.
- Is better at helping and supporting friends.
- Can be more understanding of people's feelings – feels more empathy.
- Has more emotional maturity.
- Is resourceful.

Autumn Girl
Pre-menstrual phase
Enhanced abilities and skills:

- Finds problems in everything you do and say!
- Has 'out-of-the-box' problem-solving ideas.
- Is more inspired creatively when energy levels are high.
- Can be more intuitive.
- Can argue the opposite to help her to process a problem.

Winter Girl
Menstrual phase
Enhanced abilities and skills:

- Is good at mindfulness.
- Can be insightful.
- Has a greater capacity to understand and accept the bigger picture.
- Is more able to observe and accept.
- Is better at letting go and forgiving.

As well as changes in dominant thinking, women also have four times of 'optimized' skills and abilities. 'Optimized Days' are days within a phase where they can do specific tasks better and more quickly. You may already know which skills and abilities are easier for you in particular phases, but there can also be other undiscovered talents just waiting for you to explore.

As you accompany your Daughter round her cycle you can ask her in each phase what she finds easier to do or can do more quickly. You can look at your own phases and ask yourself the same question, and perhaps compare with your Daughter – it may be that your Daughter applies her enhanced skills and abilities in ways that you have never considered. In this way you both learn together about the hidden talents within your cycles. And when you share the same enhanced skill and you are both in the same phase, how wonderful will it be to express this amazing energy and ability together?!

How understanding your Daughter's enhanced abilities and skills cycle can help

- Knowing that your Daughter has enhanced skills in particular phases means that in those phases you can tailor activities for her that will use these skills and help her to feel fulfilled and accomplished.

- Understanding her abilities means you have the benefit of her **being happy and willing** to do tasks that she finds easy and feels good at.

- Knowing that your Daughter has an aptitude for certain tasks in certain phases means that you can stop giving her things to do which she will resist. You can also have tasks that you don't want to do yourself **done quickly by someone who will love doing them and do them better than you!**

- Understanding that she has changing levels of skills means that you won't be putting **unrealistic** expectations or pressure on her to maintain the highest level of skill throughout the month. Optimised skills are a gift to use when they are given, and not to be expected all the time.

- Knowing that her optimized skills change during the month doesn't mean that she can't do any particular task, it simply means that on some days some activities will take longer or require more focus or energy or willpower. So you can give her the extra time, extra encouragement or the support that she needs, making the task easier for her to complete.

Understanding your own cycle of optimized skills and abilities also has benefits

- You will know when you have optimal planning and organising skills to create a structure and routine for your Daughter and the rest of your family.

- You will know your best time for communication and for talking to her about a difficult subject.

- You will know to leave a problem for a week so that you get a different perspective in another phase.

- You will know when specific things matter to you more or less, and you can share this knowledge with your Daughter so that she knows how to manage **you** better.

- You will know when specific things are more difficult for you, so you can delegate within the family or ask your Daughter to give you more space or time to do things.

- You will know when specific things are easier for you, so you can share with your Daughter that now is the time for her to ask you for certain activities, help or tasks.

- You will know how to manage your activities and life to make best use of your optimized skills and to feel the happiness and wellbeing that comes from matching tasks to their Optimized Days. (For more details see my book *'The Optimized Woman'*.)

Knowing about your own cyclic experiences and being open and honest about them with your Daughter not only sets a positive role model for her about managing her own changes but it also helps her to manage you! If she knows that you are pre-menstrual, then she knows that certain interactions or activities may get a stronger response from you than in the rest of the cycle. Depending on her phase she may decide to interact with you in a different way, or instead decide to have fun with confrontation!

Living closely together means that the interaction between you and your Daughter is especially important. By understanding your cyclic nature you can help to build a balanced relationship with your Daughter, because you will understand that you are expressing yourself through four different women and that **each of these women needs to create a positive relationship with her.**

The secret to feeling happy

> When you or your Daughter
> do a task in the phase where
> the appropriate abilities are enhanced,
> you can feel **fulfilled and happy!**

You now have the secret for changing your mood and your Daughter's mood. In any phase of the cycle, when you do a task which uses the optimized skills and abilities you can feel good. It may be that you and your Daughter are in different phases and need different tasks to feel good, or it may be that you are both in the same phase and doing the same task will make you both feel good.

In the present global environment, taking a little time to create a task that uses your Daughter's current enhanced abilities is a beautiful and simple way to help her to more easily manage any changes to routine and restrictions and to create feelings of wellbeing when she is experiencing insecurity and anxiety. And sharing the secret with her means that she will know that she has some control over how she feels in any phase.

THE NEEDS AND MOTIVATION CYCLE

How understanding the needs and motivation cycle can help create harmony

Summary of potential needs and motivation

Spring Girl
Pre-ovulation phase
Needs and motivation

- Being physical and wanting to be outdoors.
- Taking action.
- Starting something new.
- Feelings of achievement and accomplishment.
- Self-empowerment and control.
- Quick results.
- Learning.
- Being competitive and winning.

Summer Girl
Ovulation phase
Needs and motivation

- Being with people.
- Doing things together.
- Helping others.
- Making and supporting friendships.
- Wanting outcomes that support everyone.
- Practical creativity – physically making something.

Autumn Girl
Pre-menstrual phase
Needs and motivation

- Less tasks and more rest when energy is low.
- Activities when she is has high energy.
- Control of her time, activities and energies.
- Doing things her way.
- Projects for her critical analysis ability.
- Projects for her inspired and heightened creativity.
- Non-complex tasks for the energy lows.
- Doing things alone.
- Clearing / cleaning projects.
- Alone time when low in energy.

Winter Girl
Menstrual phase
Needs and motivation

- More time to rest and sleep.
- Time to daydream
- Withdrawal, and barriers between her and outer world problems.
- Quiet and stillness.
- Simplicity – no multi-tasking.
- A slower pace of life.
- Reduced tasks, or no tasks.
- Alone time.
- Approaches that are not superficial.
- To know that she is part of something bigger than herself perhaps a World vision.

If you know what your Daughter needs in each of her phases, you can help her to meet those needs – and then not only will you be appreciated and look 'good', you will also have a happy and approachable Daughter!

Needs are also motivation, so if you can suggest that a particular activity or task will meet one of your Daughter's phase needs then she may be more willing to give you a positive and enthusiastic response. You will be motivating her to do what you want her to do by fulfilling something she needs in the current phase. It's win-win!

It's also important that you understand **your own** needs and fulfil them, so that you can be more centred and calmer in your interaction with your Daughter. When your needs are not met, you may feel irritable and more intolerant and impatient, and you can snap at people easily. It's particularly important that you do not expect your Daughter to fulfil your needs for you.

For example, a pre-menstrual 'need' may be to declutter and create space – something that many women experience a few days before menstruation. It's not fair to expect your Daughter to clean and tidy her bedroom or personal space in order to meet this particular need in you. Instead, you can satisfy your own pre-menstrual urges by clearing and cleaning the rest of the home, and then when your Daughter is in her pre-menstrual phase you can suggest that she tidies and cleans her own space. If you make the suggestion and give her a rubbish bag when she is on a peak of energy in her pre-menstrual phase, then she is more likely to be enthusiastic about doing it!

If you both experience the same phase need at the same

time, then this can be an opportunity for you to do something that creates positive bonding – but it also has the potential to create unfulfilled needs. For example, if you are both menstrual and want to be alone and not do anything, then there could be resentment if one party is allowed to do what she needs but the other is still expected to continue to do everything 'as normal'.

Not all needs can be met, because the world doesn't let women live a cyclic life – and so compromise is needed. It could be a good idea to work out this compromise in advance, perhaps in your Daughter's ovulation phase when she can perceive the world in a more empathic way. But recognise that if you have the discussion in your premenstrual phase you may come across as demanding, and if you are in your ovulation phase you may arrange things to meet your Daughter's needs at the sacrifice of your own.

Finally, you don't have to do big things to meet your need to feel more happiness or more wellbeing. A simple little action that meets a need has as much impact as a big action! There is no need to make big life-changing decisions when a simple activity will have the same effect on you and your Daughter.

How understanding your Daughter's needs and motivation cycle can help

- Understanding and identifying your Daughter's phase needs – physical, mental, emotional, or other – and then helping her to fulfil them, will help you to look like a 'great' Mum!

- Sharing your understanding can help your Daughter to identify her own needs and to fulfil them herself. This can help her to build feelings of control while living through the chaos of hormone changes and disruptions to the environment around her.

- Understanding which actions meet her needs enables you to motivate your Daughter to do activities that can help to **lift her mood**.

- Knowing your Daughter's needs and helping her to fulfil them is a positive and proactive way for you to show **how much you love her**.

- Understanding that meeting her needs is a good way to motivate your Daughter to do particular activities or tasks enables you to ask her to do those things that you would like her to do and **get a positive response**.

- Understanding your Daughter's inner desire to express her phase-specific enhanced abilities and skills means that you have access to them – so you have the opportunity for your Daughter to be **actively involved** in tasks.

- Knowing that sometimes meeting your Daughter's needs will also be fun for you can motivate you to create the appropriate activities!

Understanding your own cycle of needs and motivation also has benefits

- If you know that meeting a phase-need motivates you, then you have the key to motivating yourself throughout your cycle!

- Knowing your own phase needs means that you can fulfil your needs yourself – without relying on someone else to make you feel wellbeing or happiness.

- If you can meet your needs and feel happier then the people around you will pick up on your mood. With the current stress that so many of us are experiencing it's important that you know how to lift your mood to keep your home environment balanced and harmonious.

- Knowing that you need to express your own enhanced abilities and skills in each phase to feel wellbeing puts more importance on giving them attention, time and space.

- Showing how **you** meet your phase needs yourself – and use them to motivate yourself to do the things you don't really want to do – offers a practical model for your Daughter on how to motivate herself.

- Sharing your own phase needs and motivations with your Daughter can help her to explore her own needs, and for you both to see where you are the same and where you are different. This can create respect for the each other's individual requirements.

- Understanding and meeting your needs can help you to create your own emotional stability and feelings of empowerment at a time when there can be many challenges from your Daughter and from the world situation.

With the stress of changes in working, employment, financial issues, insecurity about loved-ones and the future, our menstrual cycles can become irregular – or more irregular than normal. This is not unusual. There is a strong two-way interactive link between the mind and the cycle – changes in the cycle affect your mind, and what is in your mind affects your cycle. So the mental stress you hold can impact on your physical cycle and on individual phases, and it can also mean that you have stronger mental and emotional responses to your current phase. The result is that you may not be sure which of the Four Women you are currently experiencing – or which of the four Cycle-Girls you have at home!

Later in the book we will look at the impact of stress on our experiences of the four phases, but first let's see how we can become detectives and try to work out who you are and who you are living with!

CHAPTER 3
HELP! WHO IS WITH ME RIGHT NOW?

> Remember that living with a cycle is an art,
> and not a science.

The key to living with the menstrual cycle is to observe and adapt, to create and be flexible, and to flow with the energies and experiences. You may notice that your Daughter always has the same experiences in particular phases – for example, perhaps she feels increasing physical energy in her pre-ovulation phase. You may also observe that she always has the same emotional, mental, or creative experiences on particular days in each menstrual month. Perhaps you have also been teaware that your Daughter's phase experiences are influenced by what she thinks, by stress, and by the impact of the world around her.

Things could be easier for everyone if women had four

lights on their foreheads indicating their phases, but as they don't you need to be an enthusiastic observer and explorer of your own cycle and of your Daughter's cycle.

Please remember – never tell your Daughter that you think she is in a particular phase unless she asks for your insight. Keep the information to yourself, but **act on it**. Defining your Daughter by her phase can be limiting and make her feel a lack of validation for her individuality and for her experiences.

CHECKLIST FOR IDENTIFYING WHICH DAUGHTER IS IN THE ROOM WITH YOU

It's important to remember that if your Daughter's cycle is irregular she may experience phases of very different lengths to yours. This makes observation **the key** to understanding which of the four Cycle-Girls you have with you at any one time. And be prepared to make mistakes – because there will be things happening in your Daughter's life that you don't know about and which can also influence her cycle.

But there is no such thing as failure – there are just actions and approaches which are **not in alignment with the current phase**. So, try again with another approach or action.

The list of questions below is to help you to observe your Daughter and to try to make an informed guess at which of the four Cycle-Girls you currently have with you. The questions are offered simply as a guide to help you to understand the energies of your Daughter which will then give you the information needed to support her through this time of physical and world change.

And of course, you can always use the questions to help you to identify which of the four Cycle-Women you are currently experiencing yourself!

The influence of life stages

You also need to take into account the life stage of your Daughter, because this will also impact on her cyclic experiences.

The four stages of a woman's life (girl, adult woman, mature woman, elder woman) have similar energies – and enhanced abilities and needs – to the four menstrual cycle phases. While your Daughter is a young girl her energies are linear, she is growing towards a goal – and that goal is adulthood. She is developing her ego, her individuality and independence – she wants to explore the world to see what she can do and where her limits are – and she has self-belief and perhaps a long list of things she wishes to do when she becomes an adult. These energies and mindset are very similar to women in their pre-ovulation phase.

The process of changing from the child stage of life into the adult woman stage of life is gradual, and just as women go through Cycle Transition Days in their menstrual cycle, they also journey through Life Stage Transition Years. In these Transition Years they can hold some of the energies of the stage they are leaving and also the stage they are entering. The life stage influences a woman's experiences of each of the phases of her cycle, which means that throughout the cycle all phases of your Daughter can be impacted to some degree by her changes as she grows into a woman through the girl-to-woman Transition Years.

Depending on how old your Daughter is, you may find that even though she is menstrual she is still experiencing some dynamic energy. The closer to adulthood, the more likely your Daughter's cycle experiences will fit the adult generalisations below.

> Remember to be an explorer
> - to approach everything with enthusiasm,
> to watch and learn,
> and to love finding out more
> about your wonderful and beautiful
> Daughter!

Questions to ask yourself about your daughter

Physical energy questions

Tick box		Possible Cycle-Girl	Possible phase/s
	Is she physically active?	Spring Girl, Summer Girl	Pre-ovulation Ovulation
	Does her physical energy and stamina seem to be growing?	Spring Girl	Pre-ovulation

	Is her physical energy good and stable?	Summer Girl	Ovulation
	Does she seem more tired and need more rest?	Autumn Girl, Winter Girl	Pre-menstrual Menstrual
	Does her physical energy go up and down erratically?	Autumn Girl	Pre-menstrual
	Does she have long periods of activity during the day – but is then tired earlier than usual?	Autumn Girl	Beginning of the pre-menstrual
	Is she mostly tired and withdrawn but with short peaks of impulsive and compulsive energy?	Autumn Girl	Towards the end of the pre-menstrual
	Is she hibernating – sleeping more?	Winter Girl	Menstrual

Emotions and feelings questions

Tick box		Possible Cycle-Girl	Possible phase/s
	Is she emotionally stable but detached?	Spring Girl	Pre-ovulation

	Does she have continuous super-confidence in herself and in her abilities?	Spring Girl	Pre-ovulation
	Is she very positive and 'go-getting'?	Spring Girl	Pre-ovulation
	Is she ego-led?	Spring Girl, Autumn Girl	Pre-ovulation Pre-menstrual
	Is she emotionally stable?	Summer Girl	Ovulation
	Is she very loving, caring, nurturing and tactile?	Summer Girl	Ovulation
	Is she very aware of your needs and emotions?	Summer Girl	Ovulation
	Can she listen to people's problems and not get upset?	Summer Girl	Ovulation
	Does she need an emotional response from you?	Summer Girl	Ovulation
	Is she disinterested in other people's opinions or needs?	Spring Girl, Autumn Girl	Pre-ovulation Pre-menstrual
	Is she super-sensitive to anything you say?	Autumn Girl	Pre-menstrual
	Does she react explosively?	Autumn Girl	Pre-menstrual

	Is she emotionally needy?	Autumn Girl	Pre-menstrual
	Is she frustrated, intolerant, impatient or aggressive?	Autumn Girl	Pre-menstrual
	Does she seem a little low emotionally for lots of reasons?	Autumn Girl	Pre-menstrual
	Is she emotionally needy?	Autumn Girl	Pre-menstrual
	Does she withdraw emotionally for short periods of time?	Autumn Girl	Pre-menstrual in a trough of energy.
	Is she withdrawn emotionally all the time?	Winter Girl	Menstrual
	Does she seem a little low emotionally for no specific reason?	Winter Girl	Menstrual
	Is she withdrawn, but has a slight increase in positive energy?	Winter Girl transition to Spring Girl	Menstrual to pre-ovulation transition.

Perception and abilities questions

Tick box		Possible Cycle-Girl	Possible phase/s
	Does she want a reason for everything?	Spring Girl	Pre-ovulation
	Does she want structure, rules and organisation in her life?	Spring Girl	Pre-ovulation
	Does she want to do things herself?	Spring Girl	Pre-ovulation
	Is she focused on her thinking?	Spring Girl	Pre-ovulation
	Does she spend more time than usual connecting with friends	Summer Girl	Ovulation
	Is she interested in family relationships?	Summer Girl	Ovulation
	Is she focused on feelings?	Summer Girl	Ovulation
	Is she co-operative?	Summer Girl	Ovulation
	Does she show appreciation?	Summer Girl	Ovulation
	Does she want to make things?	Summer Girl	Ovulation
	Is she good at expressing herself?	Summer Girl	Ovulation

	Does she criticise everything about you and what you are doing?	Autumn Girl	Pre-menstrual
	Does she argue with everyone and every request or decision?	Autumn Girl	Pre-menstrual
	Does she have moments of high creativity followed by low emotions?	Autumn Girl	Pre-menstrual
	Is she focused on her inner imaginary world?	Autumn Girl	Pre-menstrual
	Is she drawn towards spirituality?	Autumn Girl	Pre-menstrual
	Does she have scattered creative thinking and impulses?	Autumn Girl	Pre-menstrual
	Does she withdraw from discussions or arguments?	Winter Girl	Menstrual
	Does she lack preferences? – "Whatever"	Winter Girl	Menstrual
	Is she focused inwards?	Winter Girl	Menstrual

	Does she have moments of deep insight beyond her years?	Winter Girl	Menstrual
	Is she just 'okay' – no real outward self-confidence, but no lack of confidence?	Winter Girl	Menstrual

Needs and motivation questions

Tick box		Possible Cycle-Girl	Possible phase/s
	Does she want to create order and structure?	Spring Girl	Pre-ovulation
	Does she have long lists of things she wants to do?	Spring Girl	Pre-ovulation
	Is she motivated by risk?	Spring Girl	Pre-ovulation
	Does she want to start new things?	Spring Girl	Pre-ovulation
	Does she want to begin again, no matter what?	Spring Girl	Pre-ovulation
	Is she busy?	Spring Girl	Pre-ovulation
	Does she have a desire for more?	Spring Girl	Pre-ovulation
	Does she 'want'?	Spring Girl	Pre-ovulation

	Does she want to do things on her own and her way?	Spring Girl, Autumn Girl	Pre-ovulation Pre-menstrual
	Is she motivated by controlling a situation?	Spring Girl, Autumn Girl	Pre-ovulation Pre-menstrual
	Does she want to help or to make you happy?	Summer Girl	Ovulation
	Is she very practical and happy about doing everyday things?	Summer Girl	Ovulation
	Does she want to do things with you or with others?	Summer Girl	Ovulation
	Does she enjoy doing 'home-maker' activities?	Summer Girl	Ovulation
	Does she want to take action to save the planet?	Summer Girl	Ovulation
	Does she want to help others?	Summer Girl	Ovulation
	Does she 'need'?	Autumn Girl	Pre-menstrual
	Does she need to be right?	Autumn Girl	Pre-menstrual
	Does she want to throw out old things?	Autumn Girl	Pre-menstrual

	Does she have a desire for less?	Autumn Girl	Pre-menstrual
	Is she very self-critical and want to 'fix' herself?	Autumn Girl	Pre-menstrual
	Does she have a long list of things she wants you to do?	Autumn Girl	Pre-menstrual
	Does she have compulsive ideas and creativity?	Autumn Girl	Pre-menstrual
	Does she want to do things on her own and at her own pace?	Autumn Girl	Pre-menstrual
	Is she motivated by staying inside her comfort zone and avoiding risk?	Autumn Girl	Pre-menstrual
	Can she easily identify everything that could go wrong in minute detail?	Autumn Girl	Pre-menstrual
	Will she not do something because it is 'unsafe'?	Autumn Girl	Pre-menstrual
	Does she need change?	Autumn Girl	Pre-menstrual

	Does she want to destroy?	Autumn Girl	Pre-menstrual
	Does she want to let go and give up?	Autumn Girl	Pre-menstrual
	Is she accepting of people and situations?	Winter Girl	Menstruation
	Does she want to let go but not give up?	Winter Girl	Menstruation
	Does she see the importance of saving the planet?	Winter Girl	Menstruation
	Does she want to do nothing?	Winter Girl	Menstrual

Remember that the questions in the above checklist are a simple guide to help you to observe your Daughter, and are in no way definitive. Also remember that your Daughter could be experiencing a Cycle Transition Day where she may experience a combination of the physical energies, emotions, dominant perceptions, motivation and needs, of two different phases.

If your Daughter does not seem to match any particular phase, use these checklists over a few days to see which experiences stay the same on each day – this will remove external influences (see later section below on Additional Influences) and give you a better idea of which phase she is in.

Download printable tables from *www.mirandagray.co.uk*.

Who is with me? Dial

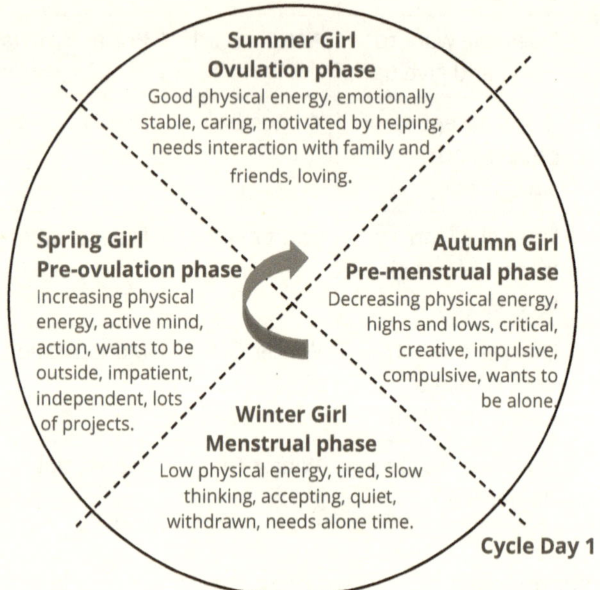

ONE SIZE DOES NOT FIT ALL!

The best way to find out which of the four Cycle-Women you currently are – and which of the four Cycle-Girls your Daughter is experiencing – is for you both to record your experiences each day. Yes, we live in a busy time! Your current life may be under more demands and stress than you have experienced before, leaving very little time for anything new. But there are huge advantages to spending just a few minutes each evening noting down your experiences and feelings. If you know who you are, then you can:

- know what your needs are and how you can meet them

- understand why you are behaving in a particular way and act to create harmony

- apply your enhanced skills and abilities to support yourself and your family

- do the things that you know are going to make you feel wellbeing and happy

- feel in control

- feel stronger

- feel less stressed and more able to manage

- feel able to wait a few days until your phase changes.

And most importantly you will **understand your needs within your relationship with your Daughter.** This will enable you to create approaches that meet both of your requirements, and thereby build a stronger, more balanced and affirming relationship.

Although your cycle can give you an insight into your Daughter's feelings, perception and energies, your Daughter's experiences are unique to her. So it's important to encourage your Daughter to also make a quick record of her experiences each day. It could be a fun activity to do this together, but if time doesn't allow then spending a little time at the end of each phase, or cycle, to share your notes and observations can help to build mutual understanding.

But how can you get your Daughter interested in starting this path of self-observation and recording? Try guessing which of the four Cycle-Girls you think she is currently experiencing and think about how you could motivate her enthusiasm and desire to be involved. Remember **to match the task to one of her skillsets or motivations,** but also think about her physical energy levels.

For example:

Spring Girl phase – she may like the approach of discovering who she is and filling in the details in the charting tables or Cycle Dials below.

Summer Girl phase – if you ask her to fill in the tables and dials *with* you, she may see this as a fun Mother-Daughter activity.

Autumn Girl phase – she may feel that the tables and dials are too restrictive, and she doesn't want to be put in a 'box'. Perhaps encourage her to find a different, more creative way in this phase to note her experiences – for example she could colour the dials or draw pictures each day.

Winter Girl phase – she may not be able to find the words to say exactly how she feels, and the logical structure of the tables may not be easy for her to think through. Perhaps say that you would like to share your own observations and to get her insight into what they may mean.

The pre-ovulation phase – Spring Girl, Dynamic Woman – is probably the best phase for starting any project because of its high levels of energy, confidence, mental abilities, and excitement over starting something new. In the Spring Girl phase your Daughter may want to record many experiences in detail. However, as the cycle changes and the dominant thinking and motivation changes, in the Summer Girl phase your Daughter may reduce the number of things she is recording and the amount of detail. In the Autumn Girl phase, she may not want to bother with recording anything, because she is more creative and connective in her thinking. And in the Winter Girl phase she may not want to record anything because everything is 'okay' and she doesn't have the energy to think and move. You may notice the same thing happens to your own recording during your month!

Living closely together can be a challenge, but it can also be an opportunity for you and your Daughter to start observing both of your energies and needs. It's a common project, with a goal of creating a better and more understanding relationship which will not only help to reduce miscommunication and disputes but also enable you both to take what you have learned about living together out into the world.

Recording your cycles

Recording your cycle experiences in tables can be a very quick and easy way for you to identify what you are feeling and experiencing. Women are generally raised in an educational mindset that teaches them to think in lists and tables, so for many women this is the easiest approach to start recording cycle observations. Also, you may not be sure what to look for, so record tables can help guide you through your observations.

But there is another possible approach using a dial rather than a table to record your experiences. You may find that your Daughter is more open to the recording tables in her pre-ovulation phase while finding the dial format more intuitive in her ovulation and pre-menstrual phase. The recording tables can appeal in the menstrual phase because they don't require too much independent thinking, but the number of questions to be answered can feel too overwhelming to process at one time. The dial approach could be more acceptable if your Daughter is comfortable with how to use it and is not recording a lot of activities, feelings and experiences each day.

Remember that the approach of this book is for you to try something, and if it doesn't work adapt it or try something completely different! There is no 'right' or 'wrong' – just things that work better in one phase than the other.

Record Table Example

The Record Tables contain lists of experiences that you and your Daughter may find helpful to record. Of course, you can record more experiences or less, depending on the phase you are in. To make things quick and easy you can just record 'Yes' or 'No', or you can give a number out of ten where '0' means you do not have the experience and

'10' means that it is very strong and impactful. There are extra blank rows for you to add your own aspects to record.

If your Daughter's phase is longer than the number of days provided, she can add extra columns to the table. If her phase is shorter, she can reduce the number of columns.

Example

Spring Girl: pre-ovulation phase

Experience	Day 7	Day 8	Day 9	Day 10	Day 11	Day 12	Day 13
	Date	*Date*	*Date*	*Date*	*Date*	*Date*	*Date*
Increasing physical energy	Yes	9	10	10	10	8	Stable
Needing less sleep	No	8	8	10	10	10	Stable
Good memory / good levels of concentration	No	3	9	10	10	10	10
Feeling energised	No	9	10	10	10	10	10
Needing to start projects and do planning	No	5	8	10	10	10	7
Self-confident	No	7	9	10	10	10	10

A month of Record tables

Download printable tables from *www.mirandagray.co.uk*

Spring Girl: pre-ovulation phase	Day 7	Day 8	Day 9	Day 10	Day 11	Day 12	Day 13
Experience	Date	Date	Date	Date	Date	Date	Date
Increasing physical energy							
Needing less sleep							
Good memory / good levels of concentration							
Thinking rationally / logically							
Outgoing and sociable							
Needing action- need to make things happen							
Feeling energised							
Needing to start projects and do planning							
Have lots of projects							
Wanting physical activity							
Self-confident							
Have positive thoughts							

Summer Girl: ovulation phase	Day 14	Day 15	Day 16	Day 17	Day 18	Day 19	Day 20
Experience	Date	Date	Date	Date	Date	Date	Date
Good physical energy							
Feeling gentler							
Feeling caring and nurturing							
Friends and family are important							
Helping others is important							
Emotionally strong and balanced							
Loving and feeling selfless							
Wanting to connect emotionally							
Practical creativity e.g. cooking							
Loving thoughts							
Able to listen							
Being patient and accepting							

Autumn Girl: pre-menstrual phase	Day 21	Day 22	Day 23	Day 24	Day 25	Day 26	Day 27
Experience	Date	Date	Date	Date	Date	Date	Date
Decreasing physical stamina							
Highs and lows in energy							
Needing more sleep							
Decreasing mental skills							
Anti-social and wanting to be alone							
Mood swings							
Emotionally sensitive							
Frustration / impatience / anger							
Creative ideas and needing to be creative							
Finding problems and criticising							
Wanting to clean and clear							
Vivid dreams / nightmares							

Winter Girl: menstruation phase	Day 1	Day 2	Day 3	Day 4	Day 5	Day 6	Day 7
Experience	Date	Date	Date	Date	Date	Date	Date
Tired and low physical energy							
Needing more sleep							
Frustrated and impatient							
Poor memory and low levels of concentration							
Feeling slow mentally and emotionally							
Withdrawn or disconnected							
Peaceful and happy to be alone							
Meditation is easy							
Day dreaming							
Un-motivated							
Accepting – 'whatever' attitude							
Feeling spiritual and intuitive							

A Monthly Cycle Dial

A Cycle Dial is a method of noting your phase experiences that makes it obvious that you are cyclic. If you write in your diary or you use tables, you can see yourself as a repeating linear pattern of different aspects. But if you record your observations on a dial, suddenly not only does it become very obvious that you are cyclic but it also makes it very easy to compare one month with another. This way you can see which days have similar experiences each month, and this means that you can **plan ahead** to meet your needs, change your workload, and take the opportunity to use your enhanced skills and abilities! Suddenly your cyclic nature no longer seems out of control. Rather than being at sea in a storm holding onto a floating tree to stay afloat amidst the changing wind and waves, instead you are in a boat with a sail and a rudder and you can navigate the storm.

It can be really important for your Daughter to feel that there is some explanation for the storm she is currently experiencing and to know that there is a way for her to have a little more control and to be able to navigate her way through it. Add a rapidly changing local and global environment, and it is more important than ever to help her to create some understanding of what is happening in her cycles and to know what she can do to support herself.

How to use a Cycle Dial

A Cycle Dial is a circle divided into as many days as you normally have in your cycle. If you have a cycle of 17 days, the circle will be divided in to 17 segments; if you have a cycle of 30 days you divide the circle in to 30 parts. Around the outside you write the Cycle Day number. The inner ring is for the calendar date. The remaining area within the segment is for you to write your short note about your experiences.

A Cycle Dial

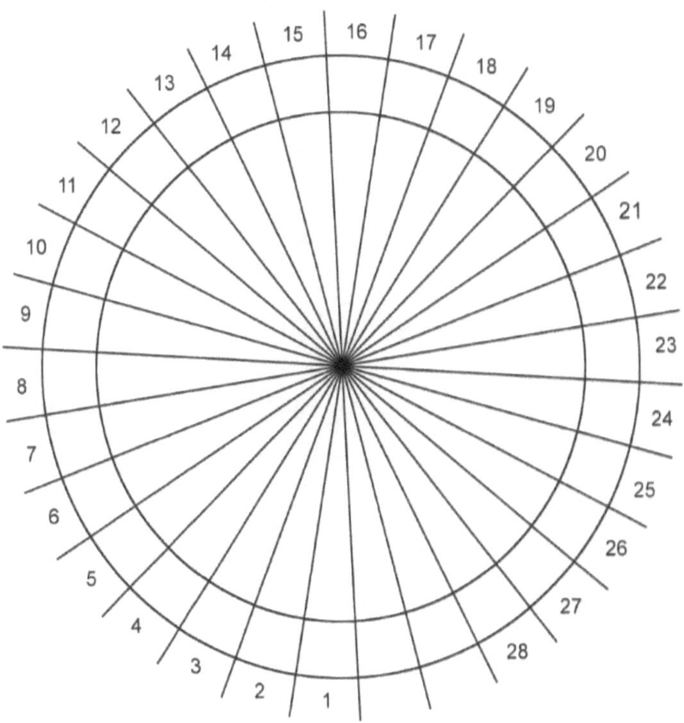

Download printable Dials from *www.mirandagray.co.uk.*

On each Cycle Day, you and your Daughter write the day's date and make a brief note of your experiences.

You can do a general Cycle Dial and just record whatever comes to mind, but this can make the dial very cluttered and difficult to read. So, it can be better to record just one aspect of yourself throughout the month – and this also makes it easier for your menstrual phase when you may only have the energy to think about one thing!

Things you can record:

- ✓ levels of physical energy
- ✓ emotional stability and sensitivity
- ✓ ways of thinking
- ✓ sociability
- ✓ activities that feel easy or hard to do
- ✓ needs
- ✓ dreams

Note: Your Cycle Dial can be clockwise or anti-clockwise – choose whichever feels right!

An example of a Cycle Dial

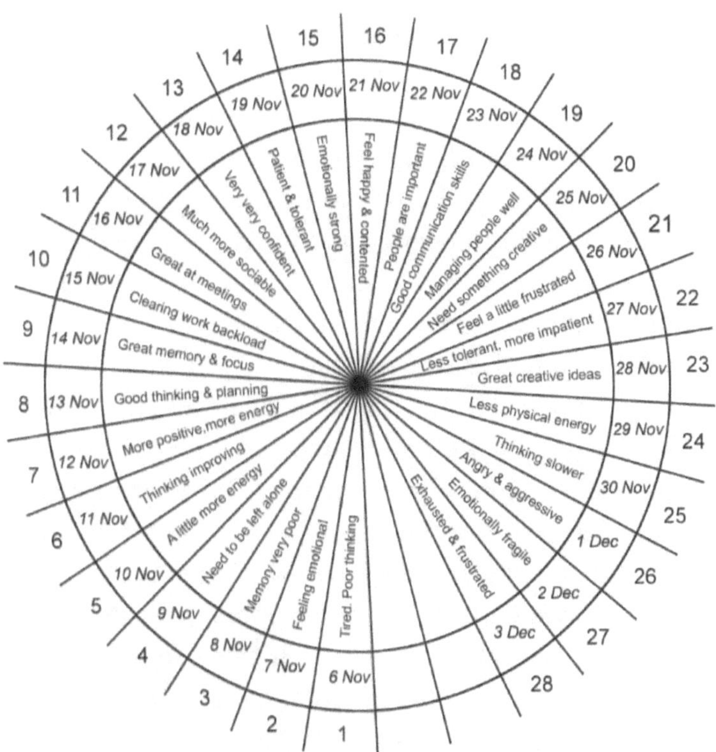

RECOGNISING EACH OTHER

It can be very helpful for everyone in your family to know which phase you and your Daughter are currently experiencing. It helps them to recognise your needs, understand why you are behaving in a particular way, and knowing what will irritate you and what will make you happy. Some women like to wear a coloured bracelet, where the colour indicates the phase they are currently experiencing. If they are experiencing Cycle Transition Days then they wear two bracelets together. It could be a lovely Summer Girl – ovulation phase – activity for your Daughter to make bracelets for you and for herself. The activity is one of practical creativity, communication and empathy (helping someone to understand her) – and of making a gift for someone else to help them.

Another way to help communicate your phases to each other and to the family is to have an area where you both stick a picture that reflects your phase. Many women use the fridge door for this, so all the family sees the pictures! Perhaps suggest that in each of the four phases your Daughter looks for photos online to find an image to represent her phase, or she may like to draw a picture. By doing the activity in each phase she will be expressing her current Cycle-Girl rather than interpreting the experience through a different perception. It's fun to see detailed paintings from the Spring Girl phase and more abstract paintings from the Autumn Girl phase.

And of course, you are going to need to do this exercise yourself so that you can place your picture on the fridge door next to hers.

Just remember to change the pictures when you feel your phase has changed and when your Daughter feels that her phase has changed.

Observing

It may be that your Daughter is not open to recording her experiences or to sharing them with you. It may be that your Daughter's cycle is very erratic, and so it's hard for her to have a sense of having a cyclic nature. In these situations you become the observer and recorder of her cycle. You could use a dial to make simple notes of her energies, her needs, what she found easy and what she found difficult, and which approaches she was positive about and which she rejected.

You can then make a summary of this information using the tables below as a way to remind yourself of the positive things that you can do to help support her, to create understanding and bring harmony, and to meet her needs to create feelings of wellbeing and happiness.

Download printable tables from *www.mirandagray.co.uk.*

What are her physical energies and stamina like? How can I help so we can enjoy them together?

Physical energies	
Pre-ovulation phase / Spring Girl	
Ovulation phase / Summer Girl	
Pre-menstrual phase / Autumn Girl	
Menstrual phase / Winter Girl	

What are her emotions like? How can I support and engage with her?

Emotions	
Pre-ovulation phase / Spring Girl	
Ovulation phase / Summer Girl	
Pre-menstrual phase / Autumn Girl	
Menstrual phase / Winter Girl	

What are her perception abilities and skills? How can we use them together to create wellbeing?

Perception abilities and skills	
Pre-ovulation phase / Spring Girl	
Ovulation phase / Summer Girl	
Pre-menstrual phase / Autumn Girl	
Menstrual phase / Winter Girl	

What motivates her and makes her feel happy? How can we both do more of this?

Motivation and 'happy' activities	
Pre-ovulation phase / Spring Girl	
Ovulation phase / Summer Girl	
Pre-menstrual phase / Autumn Girl	
Menstrual phase / Winter Girl	

What does she need from me and not need from me? How can we both create a loving balance?

Her needs	
Pre-ovulation phase / Spring Girl	
Ovulation phase / Summer Girl	
Pre-menstrual phase / Autumn Girl	
Menstrual phase / Winter Girl	

CHAPTER 4
TAKE POSITIVE ACTION: YOUR QUICK ESSENTIAL GUIDE

> The key to your Daughter's
> wellbeing and happiness
> is to create an activity
> that uses her current phase
> energies, skills and motivation, or
> that meets a current need.

When situations change, at the beginning everything can be new and a little exciting. But as time goes on and conditions may vary rapidly and radically, things that usually don't bother you and your Daughter can become bigger issues. This means that it is really important to have some quick methods of diffusing a situation and restoring balance and happiness to your relationship and to the family. Your Daughter's behaviour affects you, and your behaviour affects her, and if you have a family it will affect them as well. If you can support each other, meet each other's needs, and have fun together then little things will no longer be an issue, and you will both have the strength to take on the bigger challenges – without fighting with each other.

Below are some ideas of activities you can do with your Daughter in each phase of her cycle to help her to feel happy and fulfilled – and in return you will also feel happy and fulfilled! If you are in the same phase you can also do the same activities, so both of you feel the benefit of meeting the needs of your phase and expressing your enhanced abilities.

Obviously not all activities will be appropriate due to your situation, so use your creativity to adapt and to discover what works.

If you find that only one activity works – that's still a **great result**, because now you have an emergency fallback activity to use whenever things get difficult.

Remember – the simplest approach is to:

1. **Try something.**
2. **Observe** the outcome.
3. **Accept** that sometimes you are going to get it wrong.
4. **Change and adapt** and try again.
5. **If it works, remember to do it next time.**

SPRING GIRL: PRE-OVULATION PHASE

Summary:

Physical energy: Good, increasing.

Dominant thinking: Thinking Mind.

Heightened skills and abilities:
Planning, logic, organising,
achieving things, risk-taking, action.

Needs: Positive action, goals, achievement,
physical activity.

Quick phase-specific activities to help her to feel good

The activities suggested can be adapted to suit your circumstances and the interests and needs of your Daughter. You also need to be aware of your own phase to know how easily you can create the activities, how you can support your Daughter in doing them, and whether you feel you can be involved in them yourself.

- ✓ **Celebrate the phase!** Put a Spring Girl picture on the fridge door, ceremonially place her Spring Girl bracelet on her wrist... do something that recognises this phase.

✓ **Give her time on her own** to do what she wants to do and needs to do.

✓ **Make physical space** to enable her to do some things on her own, even if your home is small and crowded.

✓ If she is old enough, and it is safe, **let her go outside** to have exercise on her own.

✓ **Suggest starting a new exercise or dance routine** even if you don't have much room. Adapt it to your space. Make it fun! Starting something new helps meet Spring Girl's needs.

✓ **Play intellectual games** – let her play on her own, or play competitively and have a prize for the winner. Perhaps play games with a time limit for an answer, play puzzle-solving games, language or number games, and keep a winner's score list. Spring Girl has enhanced thinking skills – she is achievement orientated and she will want to win!

✓ **Play online action games competitively** – download a new one so that no one has an advantage. This will meet Spring Girl's need to learn something new and build her sense of achievement.

✓ **Give her more time and space for schoolwork.** In this phase Spring Girl will have the focus and energy she needs to catch up on learning, homework, and projects that were too difficult for her to manage in her menstrual phase.

✓ This is the time to start new projects, so suggest she starts **recording her cycle phases** using the Record Tables or the Cycle Dial.

✓ **Suggest learning a new language** (maybe choose something unusual) – spend this phase using the vocabulary you have learned together, test each other, set goals for the number of words she will each learn in a day.

✓ Suggest **action movies** – but don't force her to watch them with the family, she may want-to watch them alone.

✓ Suggest each morning that she **plans and lists what she wants to do** during the day.

✓ Suggest that she **explores things** she is interested in. She may be interested in a current issue and want to find out lots of information. This helps her to understand and process what is happening, and she may be more able interpret the figures and information in this phase.

✓ Be seen to **be responsive to her urgency**. She will expect you to drop everything and do whatever she wants. Even if you don't have the time to help immediately, validate and support her sense of urgency.

✓ **Share tasks that involve sorting things out** and creating organisation.

✓ **Ask for help with making lists and schedules** e.g. meals for the week ahead, shopping lists.

Things not to do with a Spring Girl

✗ **Don't tell her that she is becoming fixated on a subject.**
She has one phase of this super analytical power, so let her use it to fact-find and fact-check all information available.

✗ **Don't do everything for her.**
She has just come out of a phase of withdrawal during menstruation where she may have needed more help from you. Now she has energy again and she will want to use it. Help may be interpreted as you thinking that she is not good enough or able enough to manage. Remember, this is a go-getting phase with high levels of self-belief and confidence.

✕ **Don't try to keep up.**
She can be a whirlwind of energy, ideas, projects and expectations. And she will expect you to keep up! Give her space to be a whirlwind, and remember that the stream of ideas is only for one phase – by the next phase she will have settled into a more productive approach.

✕ **Don't try to contain or fight her.**
In this phase she is fuelled by urgency and the need to achieve. If she is focusing her energy on you, don't fight it – instead turn it on to something else.
'Can you make a list of…?'
'Can you find out about…?'
'Do you need extra space/time for (add activity) because I know it's important and urgent for you.'

✕ **Don't expect empathy.**
Spring Girl is the warrior, the huntress, the Amazon! She will fight to protect others and be their champion, but she will find empathy and slowing down to appreciate other people's points of view more difficult.

✕ **Don't ignore or dismiss her intellect.**
The intellect can be her dominant way of thinking in this phase and her dominant way of expressing

who she is. If you resist it, she may fight you, ignore you or go and do her own thing on her own. Being patronising in this phase is not a good idea.

Watch out for:

> **She is more willing to take risks.**
> This may not be helpful in a time of crisis. If you take an intellectual approach and tell her the facts that you have researched online, then she may be more willing not to 'do her own thing' and take a risk. In this phase appeal to her intellect rather than her sense of empathy.

SUMMER GIRL: OVULATION PHASE

Summary:

Physical energy: Good, stable.

Dominant thinking: Feeling Mind.

Heightened skills and abilities: Empathic, loving, caring for others, productive creativity, tactile.

Needs: To feel needed and included, to be able to help and support others, to be sociable, to do things as a team, and to share feelings.

Quick phase-specific activities to help her to feel good

The activities suggested can be adapted to suit your circumstances and the interests and needs of your Daughter. You also need to be aware of your own phase to know how easily you can create the activities, how you can support your Daughter in doing them, and whether you feel you can be involved in them yourself.

✓ **Celebrate the phase!** Put a Summer Girl picture on the fridge door, ceremonially place her

Summer Girl bracelet on her wrist… do something that recognises this phase.

✓ **Do activities with her!** Summer Girl is social, and any external restrictions on her meeting her friends in person can be a challenge for her. If she can't be with friends, suggest that you do some activities together.

✓ **Play games** where you sit opposite each other rather than online games, so your attention is on each other and not on a screen.

✓ **Communicate.** At the end of the day if you have both been doing different things come together and share what you have been doing. Talk to her and be a proactive listener. Share about your phase experiences and ask her to share hers.

✓ **Share your concerns.** Summer Girl is more emotionally stable and empathic, so she will be more able to understand your concerns and process them in a positive way.

✓ **Touch!** Give her an occasional and unexpected hug. Summer Girl can be tactile, and online socialising may not be enough. She may need to touch and to be touched to show love and caring.

✓ **Support her in reaching out to others.** 'Seeing' people can be very important to her, especially if she cannot meet them in person.

✓ **Help her to support others.** Summer Girl can feel the need to help others, so try to find small ways in which she can help – not just in the home but in the wider community. It can be very challenging to feel 'useless' in this phase.

✓ **Do creative projects together.** Suggest she makes a gift to give to someone – a craft project, writing a song or poem, recording a song or video. Access videos of how to make things.

✓ **Suggest cooking together** – many women like to cook in this phase!

✓ **Suggest that she arranges a special meal for the family** – draw a menu, make place names, decorate food, and everyone dresses in their 'smart' clothes.

✓ **Eat at the table facing each other** and chatting, rather than eating in front of the television or while using a phone or laptop.

✓ **Suggest online or in-person 'get togethers'** – an online tea party for her friends or a 'girls' movie night'. She is probably doing this already, but it's nice to arrange something a little more formal to celebrate this phase.

Things not to do with a Summer Girl

✗ **Don't let others take advantage of her willingness to help.**
This phase will only last about a week, and then afterwards she will have about a week of decreasing energy – and increasing frustration if she is not resting enough. If you or others give her too many on-going tasks in the Summer Girl phase – even if she is willing – there may be issues in the Autumn Girl phase.

✗ **Don't expect her to be like this forever!**
This is only one aspect of who your Daughter is. Enjoy her new perception and new enhanced skills in each phase as they can each bring depth to your relationship.

✗ **Don't expect to be left alone.**

✗ **Don't expect her to respond enthusiastically to facts and logic.**
If you want to engage her in topics, tasks, homework etc. talk about the human-interest aspect, the life-stories and the benefits to real

people and how they would be helped.

Watch out for:

> **Letting your overwhelming work and tasks destroy the relationship benefits of this phase.** Changing work practices or employment, financial priorities, social conditions and family circumstances may make increasing and often overwhelming demands on your time. But this phase can be important for your relationship with your Daughter as it's the phase in which emotional bonds are renewed and strengthened. Try to organise just a little time to show your Daughter that you love her, and to give her space to show you that she loves you. A little love in this phase goes a long way.

AUTUMN GIRL: PRE-MENSTRUAL PHASE

Summary:

Physical energy: Decreasing with peaks and troughs.

Dominant thinking: Subconscious Mind.

Heightened skills and abilities: Problem-identification, creative ideas, uninhibited thought processes, intuition, spiritual awareness.

Needs: Control, creative release, application of critical abilities, space clearing and cleaning, being alone, validation.

Quick phase-specific activities to help her to feel good

Remember what you are like in your own pre-menstrual phase.

If you find it hard to remember because you are currently in a different phase, then imagine that you have worked long hours for several days without enough sleep. You would probably be irritable, frustrated, intolerant and impatient. The pre-menstrual phase is one of decreasing physical energy and stamina, and so there is an increasing need for sleep and rest.

An irritable pre-menstrual Daughter could be an Autumn Girl who is not getting enough rest. It can also be a sign of an Autumn Girl who is trying to meet expectations, to interact with the world and to complete tasks in a manner that is not **natural,** and which is challenging for her. This can be particularly exhausting and energy-draining. Add the stress of adolescence and the changing global situation and your Daughter's responses to everyday life can be more intense. For more insight on the effect of stress on the phases see *Chapter 6: Stress and the cycle* – and the current world is stressful!

The activities suggested can be adapted to suit your circumstances and the interests and needs of your Daughter. You also need to be aware of your own phase to know how easily you can create the activities, how you can support your Daughter in doing them, and whether you feel you can be involved in them yourself.

But be aware that the effort of doing some of the activities below is worth it – because then your own current phase will be easier and calmer, enabling you to support yourself better through your own challenges.

The activities that you choose will depend on whether your Daughter is experiencing a peak of high physical energy or if she is experiencing a trough of low energy. Remember that the peaks are highest and longest at the beginning of the phase and the troughs are longer and deepest at the end of the phase. When the peaks are high she can be a whirlwind of impulsive, scattered energy, and when the troughs are deep she can be withdrawn.

Also be aware of the following:

- Energy bottled up can lead to frustration.

- Lack of sleep can lead to frustration.

- Lack of feeling loved can lead to frustration.

- Lack of a quick creative outlet can lead to frustration.

The activities below will hopefully help your Daughter to express her energies and release any frustration that could build.

✓ **Celebrate the phase!** Put an Autumn Girl picture on the fridge door, ceremonially place her Autumn Girl bracelet on her wrist… do something that recognises this phase.

✓ **Arrange for her to have more sleep and more rest** during the day. Try to give her quieter evenings, suggest she goes to bed earlier or takes powernaps during the day. Don't let a powernap go beyond 20 minutes, so suggest that she sets her alarm.

✓ **Have a designated cushion** for her to hit or squeeze when she feels frustrated and needs to release physical energy.

✓ **Don't take her backlashes and negative emotions personally.** Any restrictions may be very frustrating for her in this phase, and she may feel that she has little control over her environment. Any sharp words are her 'letting off steam'. However, if you are in your own pre-menstrual phase you may find it more challenging not to react, and you may need space on your own to process your reactions and to meet your own needs.

✓ **Give her processing time** – alone if possible – but DO NOT be seen to be giving up on her or walking away. This can feel extremely hurtful to her and may feel like being abandoned at a time of great need.

✓ **Validate, validate, validate!** This is YOUR lifesaver. Validate all her feelings, no matter how chaotic or illogical the thought processes are underneath. The subconscious is extremely quick and creative and she will utterly believe what she is thinking. Validate her feelings, but know that in a week's time she will change phase and the subject matter will no longer be so overwhelming for her.

✓ **Do not 'fix' something unless she asks you specifically.** You may think that you are helping to make her feel better, but even if it is the right thing to do you may still be in trouble for 'taking over'. Check before you do something.

✓ **Do not do nothing.** She needs to see that you care, even though she is acting like a harpy. The emotions and thoughts can be extremely difficult to control in this phase. It can be challenging for any woman to 'think' her way out of pre-menstrual experiences because the intellectual brain is not dominant, and the subconscious mind is super-fast and impactful.

✓ **Do not take personally any criticism or judgement directed at you.** Everything will blow over by the end of the phase. This is simply her super-critical, fault-finding superpower looking for a project. Try to focus her critical powers on something other than yourself, other family members or her friends – for example:

'What do you think is wrong with the layout of things in the kitchen?'

'What do you think is wrong with this text I have written?'

'Where do you think the problems are with us all keeping safe?'

Direct the critical power at something other than you, and if possible, at something useful and productive!

✓ **Help her to feel loved.** If she is low in energy, let her curl up and place a blanket around her. If she will let you, hold her until her physical tension or tears subside. Loving action, and especially loving action in the face of her frustrations and fears, is more important than saying 'I love you' because she may not believe you. But say it anyway!

✓ **Let her have 'me-time'** when she needs to be alone. Don't feel abandoned – when she is rested, she will come back into your life. And she will be more relaxed and approachable.

✓ **Help her to pamper herself.** Perhaps suggest doing something self-nurturing, especially if she is in a low energy trough and being self-critical about her body and looks.

✓ **Find quick creative projects** where she can release her creative energies easily and feel good. Print out online mandalas for her to colour, find a simple online colouring app – don't choose anything too complex, she will just get frustrated if she cannot be creative immediately.

✓ **Find ways to release the high physical frustration and tension** when she has a peak in energy – but remember the peak of energy may not last long.

✓ If your Daughter is open to spirituality, suggest she does **something spiritual.** Do simple things – say a prayer to heal the world, say prayers over the food as you cook the meal, and look online for meditations and rituals to do together.

✓ **Look out for food cravings.** These can be intense and drive women to frustration if they are not met. They can be the body's way of getting what it needs. When you can go food shopping, buy things that you know your Daughter craves in her pre-menstrual phase and keep a stock. Does she eat salty foods like crackers or popcorn, or need red meat? Does she want chocolate or ice-cream or carbohydrates? Does she often want both salty and sweet food in this phase? If you don't know, then ask her what she craves and make sure that you have some available.

Note: If she eats a normal portion and is satisfied then you know that the craving is more likely to be a physical need. If she eats more and continues to eat more, then this can be emotional eating and the ideal would be to find another activity to help her to relieve her stress.

✓ **Comfort when needed.** In a pre-menstrual energy trough, women can experience every self-doubt, self-criticism and negative thought about themselves that is stored in their subconscious.

And it can be challenging not to believe these thoughts. You Daughter may find that logic and reasoning don't change her thoughts, because the intellectual brain is not dominant. To support her through this experience, try to be comforting and caring in a way that her subconscious mind can process – through touch, through supportive and creative activity, through accepting her and not criticising her, and through being there for her when she wants you. Validate what she feels – but make sure that you are **not** validating the thought, only the way she **feels** about the thought – and validate the challenge she is going through.

✓ **Offer Kleenex and comfort when she is upset and crying.** Create a safe, non-judgemental space for her to cry. Acknowledge her upset and ask if she feels that she needs comfort or space alone.

Things not to do with an Autumn Girl

✗ **Don't tell her that it's not real and to snap out of it.**

✗ **Don't be impatient and exasperated.** DO NOT walk away in a manner that could suggest that you are giving up on her or abandoning her. Yes, it's a challenging situation, but these actions could add fuel to the fire – which can mean that it will take longer for you to return to a harmonious relationship. If the situation has gone beyond fixing, then you need to wait until the hormones change to the next phase.

✕ **Don't be super-positive and bouncy when she is low** to try to pull her out of any low emotions. Perhaps you are in your Dynamic phase with lots of energy and positive belief – and less empathy! Being super-positive could create more negative feelings, but being gently positive and caring and steering her slowly towards a positive action that she will enjoy can help.

✕ **Don't believe everything she says about you and your relationship.** She is simply expressing old patterns, fears, beliefs and experiences that lie in her subconscious. She is responding from the past, not from the present, to release all the old emotional baggage that she no longer needs to carry – but still does. Any crisis will increase the release of old fears, patterns and emotions. This is 'processing', and it's important processing for her to be able to balance who she is.

✕ **Don't tell her that she is pre-menstrual and acting irrationally.** NO woman wants to hear this. She doesn't want someone very close to her and trusted to pigeonhole her into a restricted view of what she should or shouldn't be or tell her how she should or shouldn't behave. The Autumn Girl wants to be free to be who she is without barriers and constraints. Validate her wildness, tell her how much you love being with the free and magical young woman she is right now. Say that you will walk this 'up and down' path with her no matter what happens because you love and respect this magical aspect of herself.

✗ **Don't tell her how she should behave based on what you have read in this book!**

✗ **Don't quote from this book!**

✗ **Don't tell her what to do** – suggest only, and give her extra time to process the suggestion.

✗ **Don't criticize or judge her** – even if you are also pre-menstrual. Find your own critical superpowers a safer project to focus on!

✗ **Don't do things for her without checking first** – don't take over, especially if you are in your pre-ovulation or ovulation phases.

✗ **Don't think you can 'fix' it** – there is nothing to 'fix' and everything to experience, express and to learn from.

✗ **Don't feel that you can't do anything right.** The likelihood IS that you can't do anything right at the moment, but don't give up! A wrong action or approach is simply information, so use it to try a different approach or make a note for the next month. Every month you have an opportunity to find out more about your Daughter and yourself. It is a growing relationship, a dance that changes tempo and steps. Enjoy this beautiful and creative and magical dance!

Watch out for

➢ **Having intense talks about what is wrong with your relationship.**
NO, NO, NO! Don't let her focus her critical superpowers on you, on herself or on your relationship.
Instead try to steer the conversation to critical analysis of something else. However, be subtle – if you are too obvious, she may feel you're changing the subject and dismissive of her concerns or exhibiting a lack of validation of her feelings. The reaction to this could be anger or hurt.
But let her talk, as this is her subconscious

processing her feelings. Just make sure that you acknowledge that you are listening.

Important for when the tears fall

The Autumn Girl may not seem to have empathy and compassion when she is criticising you and finding every little fault, but actually there is a very raw empathy which often surfaces in her troughs of physical energy. In this phase your Daughter may feel everything personally. When she's watching a moving news report, she's not just feeling sad for the people in distress – instead she can respond with such an enormous amount of empathy that she feels **their distress as her own**. There is no separation, just the raw emotions of the person she is seeing as if they are hers. This is why so many women don't watch the news in the pre-menstrual phase – it is too emotionally overwhelming for them. And if you notice your Daughter – or yourself – crying at a chick-flick or a cartoon, this is also an expression of the same ragged empathy!

To make things even more interesting, the dominant subconscious mind responds to the surge of emotional empathy by bringing up the feelings of every past event in your life where you have experienced similar emotions. As a teenager your Daughter is learning to process adult emotions, so this process can be very challenging for her – and it's not exactly easy for experienced Cyclic Women! Unresolved emotions of the past also become part of our current empathic experience, increasing the emotional overload in this phase. It's no wonder that women cry a lot in this phase – crying is a safe way to express and to release this staggering emotional overload. Ultimately the reason for this emotional upsurge is to help women to release their emotions so that they don't carry them as baggage into the next month. But it can feel devastating, especially at times of global crisis. Imagine what it must be like not to have your own life experience to help you through the challenges of this phase, and in addition to have your feelings intensified by adolescence and distressing events. It is not surprising that your Daughter's pre-menstrual phases may be more intense.

Although she doesn't have cyclic experience, you do – and you can be there to support and protect her sensitive empathic nature. Make sure she has enough rest and alone time, somewhere that makes her feel safe. Perhaps protect her from too much information about the outside world so that she has less to react to emotionally and is more able to process what she does feel. Don't try to fix things – instead 'hold' space for her to be who she is. Perhaps also share the activities that you do in your pre-menstrual phase to help you to sail your boat through the stormy seas. Be there for her when she is crying and offer simple validation of her feelings and comfort. Be strong, stable, and gentle. Very often, even she won't know why she is feeling so emotional about a silly story she has heard, but **you** do – she is an amazing young woman with super-empathic powers and dominant subconscious thinking.

After she has cried, she may be exhausted – so let her sleep to restore her energies.

As your Daughter nears menstruation, you may notice

that her emotions start to become more stable. The intense empathy created through **identification** lessens, and in the menstrual phase it is replaced by empathy with **love**, where love is the strengthening and stabilising emotion. Just remember that Winter Girl doesn't always appear on the first day of menstruation – she can appear a few days before or after.

WINTER GIRL: MENSTRUAL PHASE

Summary:

Physical energy: Low and stable.

Dominant thinking: Deep Mind.

Heightened skills and abilities: Intuitive, inner-knowing, big picture vision, identification of core values.

Needs: Rest, quiet and stillness, simplicity, slower pace of life, withdrawal, alone time, to be in harmony with her life path.

Quick phase-specific activities to help her to feel good

Now think about how you are in your menstrual phase. If you find it hard, then imagine that you have worked long hours without enough sleep for so long that your mind and body say 'enough' and force you to rest and recover. You let go of everything because all you can do is sleep. If you must be active, you are slow to think and move, and you have to decide if something is important enough to get you out of bed.

Now you know what your Daughter is feeling!

The activities suggested here can be adapted to suit your circumstances and the interests and needs of

your Daughter. You also need to be aware of your own phase to know how easily you can create the activities, how you can support your Daughter in doing them, and whether you feel you can be involved in them yourself.

- ✓ **Celebrate the phase!** Put a Winter Girl picture on the fridge door, ceremonially place her Winter Girl bracelet on her wrist… do something that recognises this phase.

- ✓ **Rest, Rest, rest!** In this phase let your Daughter sleep more and take powernaps when she needs them.

- ✓ **Let her wear comfortable clothes** and, if she wishes, to 'wear' a duvet or a blanket!

- ✓ **Reduce the noise and the impact of the outside world.** Help her to set and maintain some distance between news, family issues and friends' emotions and anxieties. Ask the family to be less noisy around her. Let her wear headphones / earbuds / earplugs to help lessen the impact of the outer world. Let her keep the curtains drawn, or the blind down, to create a safe dark sanctuary away from the world.

✓ **Reduce the number of physical tasks** she needs do, ideally until she has more energy but at least for the first 2-3 days.

✓ **Tell family members** that she is having a few days resting more, that she may be a little less active on social media, but that all is well. This reduces the pressure on her to manage other people's issues and emotions.

✓ **Reduce the amount of thinking tasks** she needs to do. Her intellectual thinking may be slower, and tasks can take longer. Multi-tasking can create added stress and the potential of overwhelm.

✓ **Understand** that when she changes into the Spring Girl she will need less sleep, be able to do more and to **catch up** on tasks that have been left.

✓ **Suggest that she does gentle activities – watching movies or TV series, listening to music, or reading books.** Let her curl up. Let her choose if she wants you with her, family members with her, or if she wants to be alone.

✓ **Give her space to daydream.** Don't expect interaction from her all the time.

✓ **Accept that she is going to be withdrawn.** This doesn't mean that you have done something wrong, or that she is depressed – it's simply because she is managing limited reserves of energy.

✓ **Help her to decide what is 'urgent' for her to do,** and what can be left for a few days. She may want to give up everything, so helping her to delegate will enable her to meet her own needs, the urgent needs of others, and schoolwork deadlines.

✓ **Be loving and reassuring.** You don't need to 'do' anything, just being there can be enough.

Things not to do with a Winter Girl

✗ **Don't expect her** to be outgoing and sociable.

✗ **Don't expect her** to be interested in the outside world.

✗ **Don't expect her** to have the same physical energy and stamina that she has in other phases.

✗ **Don't expect her** to want to be with you.

✕ **Don't push her** into doing things she doesn't want to do, or that she doesn't have the energy to do. Willpower uses up energy fast, so if she is forcing herself to do something at a time when she already has low energy she will use up all her resources more quickly.

Watch out for:

➢ **Not getting enough rest.**
The menstrual phase without enough rest can feel similar to sleep deprivation. If you don't get enough sleep your body doesn't have time to heal, your mind doesn't have the time it needs to process, and you don't restore your energies – so you can't bounce back into the world in the morning. Withdrawal in the menstrual phase is important for wellbeing. If women don't get enough sleep in this phase, they can experience a slower increase in physical and mental energy in the pre-ovulation phase. When women are constantly over-riding their menstrual needs, they can find themselves experiencing low energies throughout the entire month – regardless of the phase they are in.
As your Daughter's body and mind are growing and developing, her menstrual needs are more intense, and so giving her rest time in her menstrual phase is important. By being allowed to withdraw, by being giving more control over

meeting her needs, she will begin to learn for herself the benefit of menstrual withdrawal and experience the enhanced gifts within the phase. The hope is that as she enjoys this menstrual experience she will continue to strengthen her wellbeing in adulthood by making menstrual rest an important routine in her life, whatever her work or circumstances.

CHAPTER 5
HARMONIOUS COMMUNICATION

CREATING A PRACTICAL LANGUAGE

It's important to find a 'language' that you can use to quickly recognise your experiences of each phase and to be able to share them with others in a way that can help them to understand. This language does not necessarily need to be words like 'Spring Girl' and 'Loving Woman', it can be made from images, objects, ideas and sensations. It can be much easier to explain how you feel by saying 'I am like a cat today – I want to sleep more in the sun and do less. I like to be gently stroked – but if you irritate me, I will hiss and scratch' than it is to say 'I am in my pre-menstrual phase, my physical energies are decreasing, I need more sleep to stop me from being irritable, and my subconscious mind is dominant so I may view normally appropriate approaches as intrusions and respond negatively'!

Describing who you are

You may like to suggest to your Daughter in each of her phases that she describes who she is by answering the questions below – and in return, you could answer them as well. This is a beautiful way to discover who your Daughter is and how she views herself in each phase. There are no 'right' or 'wrong' answers, and the 'language' may change as she grows, or as outside influences shape her cycle and herself. It is also a beautiful mirror to hold up to yourself in each of your phases to answer the question, 'who am I?'

Remember that in Cycle Transition Days you and your Daughter may experience qualities from two phases at the same time.

- **Which animals describe and express who you are at the moment?**
  Perhaps you are like a highly active bird – or you are a bird that glides on the wind? Maybe you are like a whale floating in the deep ocean, or a bear hibernating during the winter? Perhaps you are like the opportunistic fox, or the wise owl? Maybe you are a spider creating beautiful webs, or a butterfly flying aimlessly between flowers, or a cat focused on a mouse?

- **What colours best describe who you are? And what colours would you like to wear?**
  Are you called to bright electric colours or soft pastels? Perhaps you want natural colours rather

than synthetic colours. Maybe you want hot oranges and yellows, or warm pinks and reds, or dark purples and black.

- **What scent describes you, and what would you like to wear?**
  Are you attracted to light floral scents, or deeper notes of wood tones? Do branded perfumes call to you, or do you prefer natural essential oils?

- **Which of the four elements represents you?**
  Earth as mountains, or flat plains, or deep caves? Water as rain, or small streams or lakes, or vast oceans? Fire as a candle flame, the warm cooking fire, or the out-of-control forest fire? Air as the gentle breath during sleep, the soft cooling breeze, the hot winds of the desert, or the destructive hurricane and tornado?

- **What type of woman describes and expresses who you are?**
  A playful child, a flower fairy, a princess, a mermaid, a warrior, a huntress, a scholar, a queen, a mother, a teacher, an earth fairy, a guardian, a companion, a magician, an enchantress, a dark fairy, a dark warrior, a wise woman, a grandmother, an old witch, a meditating woman, a sleeping woman?

- **What types of clothes and fabrics describe and express who you are?**
  Imagine that you have been given an unlimited budget and you do not need to follow fashion! Do you want to wear tight clothes that show your body or sporty clothes – or perhaps fairy wings and flowers? Perhaps you want to wear floral prints and soft materials. Do you want to wear modern clothes or long medieval dresses? Maybe you want to go Goth and witchy with dark clothes, or simply want to wear old PJs and a duvet? Wearing nothing is also an option!

If your Daughter likes drawing, she could draw an illustration of herself showing the different clothes and colours she would like to wear in the phase. She could draw herself in a landscape with her animals. You could put the picture on the fridge door when she is in the phase as a lovely way to remind her of who she is – especially when the everyday world tries to treat her as the same person throughout the month.

The exercise above can also be a way for her to choose something to wear in each phase to communicate who she is. Perhaps she has hair slides in four different colours, or four different earrings, tee-shirts, night clothes, bags, purses, phone covers or keyrings… These objects are a way for her to announce who she is, but they are also a way to remind her that she could be feeling things and behaving in a particular way because she is in a specific phase. They can also be a reminder to do the actions that meet her phase needs and express her enhanced abilities and dominant thinking – because they can generate feelings of happiness and wellbeing. To get her involved, make the benefits to her very, very obvious.

And, of course, you can express your own phase, so that when your Daughter sees that you are wearing a specific pair of earrings, or she smells your chosen perfume, or notices you are wearing a particular colour, or that your phone's ringtone has changed, then she will know who you are without you having to tell her. But don't forget the teenage super-ability to ignore everything even if it is very obvious!

> **The secret** to getting her involved is
> to show her the **benefits** to herself.

THE KEY TO GETTING A 'YES' RESPONSE FROM YOUR DAUGHTER!

An important key for living in harmony is **communication**. Communication with your Daughter is communicating with a Cyclic Woman, so at any one time you could be connecting with one of four different Cycle-Girls – and remember, they all think in different ways and have different needs.

This means that if you want a positive and enthusiastic response from your Daughter to your suggestions, you need to be able to phrase them in a way that meets the needs, energies and motivation of her current phase. If you do not know which of the four Cycle-Girls is currently sharing your home, then you need to phrase your suggestion in four different ways – one for each of the Girls – to get at least one 'yes' response.

The key to any approach is to think about your Daughter's current:

- levels of physical energy

- dominant thinking

- enhanced abilities and skills

- needs and motivation.

Then you need to find something about the activity you are requesting that will meet one or more of these aspects of your Daughter's current phase.

An example of adapting your request

The request: The home needs cleaning, and you would like her to help you.

An approach for a Spring Maiden

Ability and motivation used: Organisation, physical activity, and achievement. Increasing levels of physical energy.

You could say to your Daughter that it might be a good time to get a little more organisation and structure about where you put things in the home. Suggest lots of physical and mental activities, and present a list of tasks which she can tick off as they are completed. You may like to give a goal of getting particular areas cleaned by a certain time and remind her of the countdown the closer you get to the 'high-five' moment of achievement.

An approach for a Summer Girl

Ability and motivation used: Nurturing and practically helping others. Good stable levels of physical energy.

For the Summer Girl your approach could be to say how nice it feels to be in such a lovely home, but **you** would feel happier and more comfortable if things were a little tidier. Take some time first to talk about how the home could be made better for everyone living in it, and what activities she could do to make it feel more caring. Perhaps 'reward' yourselves afterwards by making something nice to eat to share with the family.

An approach for an Autumn Girl

Ability and motivation used: To clean, declutter and create space. Variable levels of physical energy. You could ask your Daughter if she feels a little frustrated by the mess and by not being able to find things easily. As long as she is on a physical energy high when you approach her and she is not totally focused on something else, you could suggest that it would be fun to do a 'mega clean'.

Your Daughter is going to need a little help with direction and management. First, watch her energy levels; if they drop, let her rest a little and have something to eat and drink. Don't force her against the energy low or she will react. Secondly, focus her energies on specific tasks, or her scattered energy will go everywhere and make more mess not less. Give her a specific area or room or task. Do not give her anything to do that involves discernment – she will just throw out everything!

A Winter Girl approach

Ability and motivation used: Not doing much physically, wanting rest and peace.

Your approach could be to say how much more peaceful and restful the home would feel if it was clean and tidy. Suggest that she could do small, simple tasks with breaks. Don't ask her to do the very physical tasks and, if she wishes, allow her do things on her own at her own speed. You may not get everything done that you want, but you will have her helping. Perhaps wait a week and then ask for help with the more physical tasks!

> If you are not getting a positive response to your approaches, go back to your observations about her cycle and look for ways you can match the task to her energies, enhanced abilities and needs – these will provide you with the key to motivating your Daughter.

FOUR SIMPLE APPROACHES TO GET A 'YES' RESPONSE!

If you know the phase that your Daughter is in, and you know from your observations how her energies and dominant thinking and needs are expressed in that phase, then you can tailor any question in a way that will be accessible, approachable and agreeable to her.

For example, if she is Spring Girl then use intellectual and logical language, talk about activity and achievement. If she is Summer Girl use an emotional approach, talk about feelings and caring for others. If she is Autumn Girl, then focus on identifying problems, or wild creative ideas, or about her intuitive feelings. And if she is Winter Girl, use gentle language, talk about accepting and allowing things to flow, talk about rest, and maybe offer a spiritual or 'wider vision' approach.

Obviously, your approach will be unique to your relationship with your Daughter and to her expression of her phases, but here's an idea of the types of approach:

Activity: Using the recycling bins

Spring Girl – How many different things can we recycle? Would you like to be in charge of recycling? Do you think we can recycle all our paper each week? What do you think is the best way to do this?

Summer Girl – There is so much plastic in the oceans that sea creatures are dying, we need to help them. Let's draw a 'thank you' message on the recycling containers to say thank you to everyone who recycles. Recycling is a way for us to show that we care about everyone and all animals.

Autumn Girl – Look at this rubbish, it needs to be cleared away and recycled. It's going to be very satisfying to sort through the rubbish, put it in the containers and have it taken away. You can even do it sitting on the floor if you feel tired.

Winter Girl – We all need to save the planet. If everyone did something small to help, then we could change things for the better. We are all part of this planet, linked together. Let's show that we love this world and recycle our everyday rubbish in the bins. Would you like to help? You don't have to do much, just put your own rubbish in the right bin.

If you find that you are not getting a positive response, then take a month and observe how your Daughter's energies, skills and needs motivate her in each phase. Then use this knowledge to approach her in the best way to get a positive and enthusiastic response.

Remember that this is not a science, it's a dance – and different things can affect the dance steps. Again, you can use your own cycle experiences as a guide, but please remember that your Daughter is not you and she has her own unique experiences and circumstances in which to explore and discover her cyclic nature.

Yes, it will take you time and effort to find the best approaches – but the reward is a more understanding and calmer relationship at a time when circumstances are stressful.

Checklist for your request

	Yes / No
Does your request meet her current physical needs?	
Are you using an approach and words that match her dominant thinking?	
Does the request in some way use her enhanced abilities and skills?	
Does the request meet one of her needs?	
Is the request in alignment with her current motivation?	

The more of these boxes that you can mark with a 'yes', the more likely you are to get a positive and enthusiastic response to your request.

If you still get a 'no', then try again. Change your language, change the approach, notice what she says when she responds with a 'no' and adjust your proposal.

Four simple approaches

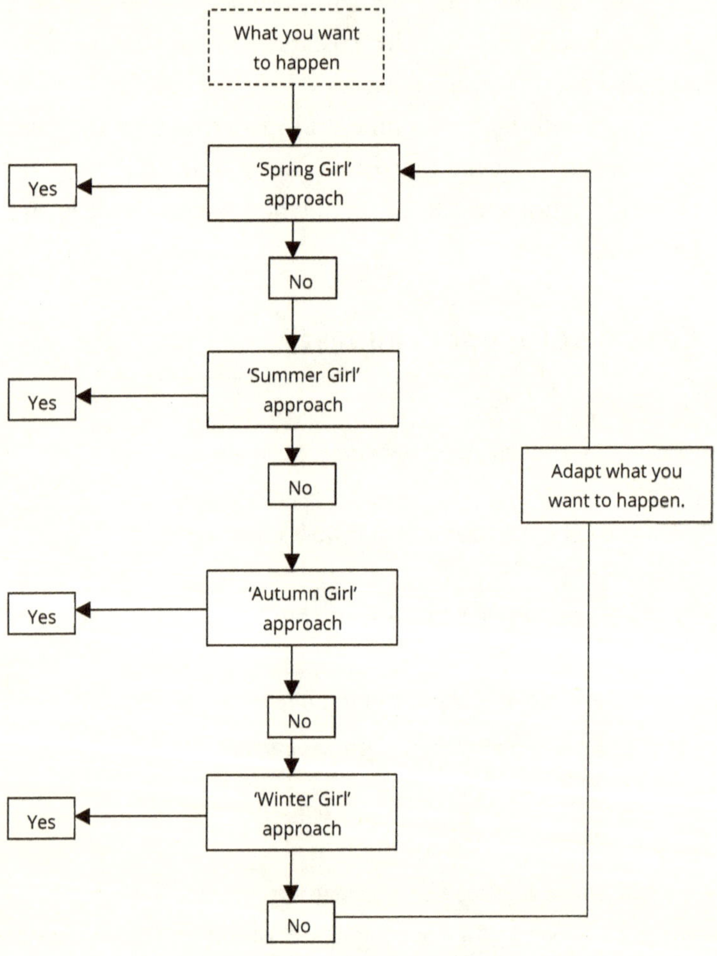

Quick guide to communicating with the four Cycle-Girls

Does your approach match her current needs?	
	Needs
Spring Girl Pre-ovulation	Action, intellectual expression, physical activity.
Summer Girl Ovulation	Creating win-win situations, emotional communication, creating positive relationships, sharing and helping others.
Autumn Girl Pre-menstrual	Energy release / withdrawal, creative expression, freedom, space, control.
Winter Girl Menstrual	Withdrawal, rest, reflection time, peace, time alone, spiritual time.

Does your approach match her current perception?	
	Perception
Spring Girl Pre-ovulation	Details, structure, logic, intellectual, learning, concentration.
Summer Girl Ovulation	Empathy for emotions and feelings, altruism, compassion, caring, emotional connection.
Autumn Girl Pre-menstrual	Highly creative, inspired, scattered, intuitive, problem identification, creative problem solving.
Winter Girl Menstrual	The bigger picture, inner knowing, acceptance, allowing, spiritual.

Does your approach match her current motivation?	
	Motivation
Spring Girl Pre-ovulation	Personal achievement, personal growth and success.
Summer Girl Ovulation	Helping and caring for others. Working together for a common outcome.
Autumn Girl Pre-menstrual	Removing the old, creating space, having control, being creative. Rest when needed.
Winter Girl Menstrual	Simplicity, rest, peace, doing things slowly, alone-time.

Communication based on her
dominant thinking and current
motivation is key to a
peaceful and happy relationship.
And you are more likely
to receive a positive response.

CHAPTER 6
STRESS AND THE CYCLE
– AND THE CURRENT WORLD IS
STRESSFUL!

Outside influences can have a significant effect on women's cycles, perhaps increasing or decreasing the length of their cycle and also changing the emotional, mental and physical experiences of the different phases. Currently the world is very stressful, and can be a rapidly changing and potentially threatening environment.

Stress overwhelms the subtle changes in thinking with a 'fight or flight' response. Mother Nature doesn't want women going up to a tiger with Dynamic Woman risk-taking curiosity or with Loving Woman empathy – Nature just wants them running away as fast as possible! Stress floods the body with chemicals, and in this hyper-alert state the subtle aspects of women's cyclic nature are pushed to one side so that they can either fight against the situation or run away to safety. In short-term periods of stress this response is very important and appropriate, but in situations where threats could continue for many months or years maintaining the 'fight or flight' response is not healthy for the body and mind, or for relationships.

You probably already know how you feel and behave when stressed – being sharp in communication, avoiding help, being more direct or aggressive, crying more often, being less empathic and more focused on yourself and what you need, being more controlling, and perhaps being less loving and less willing to be touched or to have some-one close.

If you imagine a pre-menstrual woman, you have an image of a woman under stress. This pre-menstrual stress usually comes from a society not enabling women to easily meet the needs of their cyclic nature. When there is stress from not meeting pre-menstrual needs PLUS stress from a crisis, then the pre-menstrual phase can be particularly challenging.

To look after your own wellbeing, to help you to maintain your balance, and to create a positive relationship with your Daughter throughout each month during a time of crisis or anxiety, it's important to recognise how stress can manifest in each of your Daughter's four phases. It's also important to look at the four Cycle-Women within you, to see how you express your own stress in each of your four phases. Remember this is a dance – your cycles are weaving together, and your cycle will affect your Daughter's dance and hers will affect yours.

THE STRESSED SPRING MAIDEN

The Spring Maiden in 'fight or flight' mode becomes more ego-focused, more direct, and more domineering, and she finds security in things being done in exactly the way she wants – usually with rules and structure. She doesn't trust anyone except herself to do things correctly, and she expects everyone to strictly follow the rules.

But the insecurity of a constantly changing world and varying societal requirements in everyday life means that she can become more rigid in her attempt to control things and to create structured meaning. The chaos of the lack of predictability of the usual routine and the lack of personal freedom to be independent and away from the family can create a very stressful environment for Spring Girl.

You can help your stressed Daughter in her pre-ovulation phase – and help her to respond to any crisis or anxiety in a balanced way – by trying one or more of the Spring Girl activities in the chapter *Take positive action: you quick essential guide,'* or by suggesting that she reads the Spring Girl Meditation at the end of this chapter.

THE STRESSED SUMMER GIRL

The Summer Girl in 'fight or flight' mode tends to define herself by actively helping others, and in this way she can alleviate her fears. This can make her–bossy and very controlling due to her fears for the safety of you, her family and her friends. A short period of super-active Summer Girl can be essential to get through a crisis situation, but she only has these energies for the ovulation phase and then she is in the declining physical energies of the pre-menstrual phase. Make sure that your Daughter doesn't promise too many things to help others.

The Summer Girl needs relationships and personal connections and to feel that she is part of a group or a community. Online chat and groups can help towards this, but the ovulation phase needs can be more tactile, and in-person relationships are a source of wellbeing as well as self-identification. Because of restrictions she may not be able to be with her friends, so time on social media is very important to her wellbeing and may increase in this phase.

Where the intellect may be important to the Spring Girl, feelings and touch can be very important to the Summer Girl, and a pandemic with 'no touch' constraints can be very impactful to her sense of wellbeing.

To help create a positive relationship so that you are both responding to the crisis in a balanced way, try one or more of the Summer Girl activities in the chapter *'Take positive action: you quick essential guide,'* or you may like to read her the Summer Girl Meditation at the end of this chapter.

THE STRESSED AUTUMN GIRL

The Autumn Girl in 'fight or flight' mode can express a lot of anger and frustration at enforced limitations and at the lack of freedom to do what she wants 'her' way. The Autumn Girl needs to know that she has control, because she herself is going through often unpredictable daily changes. As she slows down physically and mentally she can increasingly need to control the environment and the people around her so that she can manage everyday life without becoming overwhelmed – and consequently feel more safe and secure. So the Autumn Girl needs the freedom to rest when she is tired, and the freedom to drop excess tasks and responsibilities that drain her energy resources.

The Autumn Girl may also have a super-sense of danger, which in a crisis or unfamiliar situation can become overstimulated. This superpower is extremely useful for keeping her safe, but she may need some help with working out the actual level of risk. She may see everything as equally 'dangerous' and can become very domineering and independent when her concerns are not validated or considered.

The Autumn Girl may also have a strong impulse to clean which can release anxiety – but it has the potential to become out of proportion. She may also have a strong compulsive need to understand everything and a need to 'fix' everything – including herself.

This can be a particularly challenging phase – try several of the Autumn Girl activities in the chapter *'Take positive action: you quick essential guide,'* and also read *'Important for when the tears fall'* – and perhaps suggest the Autumn Girl Meditation at the end of this chapter.

THE STRESSED WINTER GIRL

Winter Girl in 'fight or flight' mode can withdraw very

deeply, and people around her can interpret this with-drawal as her being unloving and uncaring. This can lead to misunderstanding and feelings of insecurity in both parties. A stressed Winter Girl may feel detached from the world, unable to motivate herself or to seek help when she needs it.

Although rest is very important and necessary for well-being in this phase, when it is out of balance it can become an escape, and she may need help to find a better way of managing and processing the situation.

A stressed Winter Girl can also find it hard to recognise a bigger meaning to a situation and will need help to re-frame things in a positive way. If you have a spirituality, philosophy or religious belief, sharing this can help her to make sense of things and to feel safer and more empow-ered to step back out into the world.

The unbalanced Winter Girl can also lose her ability to be patient and to accept, and she can scatter her limited energies in trying to 'fix' her feelings. Without balance, Winter Girl may fear that she will be in these energies for-ever, and she may need help to look towards the coming of the Spring Girl phase with hope.

To help your Daughter to stay connected to the outer world in an affirming and interactive way – try one or more of the Winter Girl activities in the chapter '*Take positive action: you quick essential guide,*' or suggest she reads the Winter Girl Meditation at the end of this chapter.

MEDITATIONS FOR HELPING TO BALANCE STRESSED CYCLE-GIRLS

The subconscious mind can't tell the difference between outer reality and the inner reality of your imagination. So although physically you may be restricted, in your mind you are free to create the experiences that you need! This means that if your Daughter is feeling unbalanced in her phase, you can help her to meet her needs and to express her energies by guiding her on visualising positive and helpful scenarios. You can make up stories and meditations tailored to your Daughter, or you could use one of the meditations below as a starting point. And of course, you can also use these meditations for yourself!

Spring Girl (Pre-ovulation phase) Meditation

Societal expectations, changing technologies, and your personal domestic situation can result in different restrictions, regulations, and social conventions. An inability to easily express the renewed dynamic physical energies of the Spring Girl pre-ovulation phase in this environment can create feelings of frustration and trapped energy, and of being constricted. Spring Girl needs to be outside and free!

Your Daughter may be in a situation with limited physical freedom, but she can let Spring Girl free in meditation to feel her energies and to express them. And the more detailed you make the visualisation the happier Spring Girl will be — because you will also be exercising her intellectual powers of hyper-attention. So, if you are reading the following meditation to your Daughter, add lots of extra details to the images.

> To help create a balanced pre-ovulation phase, read the Spring Girl Meditation **in the phase**.

A Spring Girl Meditation

Preparation:

You don't need to have anything specific for this meditation, but it's nice to have an image or an object that represents the energies and experiences of Spring Girl / the pre-ovulation phase / the increasing Moon. Your Daughter may also wish to wear something that expresses her Spring Girl energies.

Meditation

Close your eyes and take a deep breath.

(Pause)

Imagine that the sun is above you in a clear blue sky.

Feel the warmth of the sunlight on your face.

Feel, know or see that you are standing on top of a rounded hill.

Beneath your bare feet the grass is green and soft.

Above you the sky is a beautiful blue, and you see birds high above playing in the breeze.

In front of you is a landscape of gentle green hills, of small woods and flower-filled fields.

You take a deep breath and reach out your arms either side of you and feel free.

In your mind, say 'I am free!'

(Pause)
You feel soft feathers extending out from your arms and fingers. And you stretch your arms and wings outwards.

Let go of the tension of holding yourself in, of being small or confined.

You are now free, and as big as the horizon.

Take another deep breath.

Let go.

Be free to be who you are.

Stretch your wings out even further, feel energy, joy and happiness flowing through you. This is who you are.

(Pause)

You start to walk down the hill alongside a small stream flowing between the trees. The wind moves the leaves, and they rustle as you walk beneath them.

But walking isn't enough to express the joy that you feel, and so you start to run and dance and jump!

You feel the rhythm of your feet on the earth, the sun above you and the wind around you. As you run and dance you relax into the rhythm and feel your connection to the Earth and to Mother Nature.

All is good.

All is well.

Your body moves with freedom and happiness!

(Pause)

You run through the meadows of small yellow, pink and blue flowers, until you stop once again at the top of a hill.

Stretch your **physical** arms out as far as they will go, with your palms facing upwards, and feel your wings expand.

Feel the energy of your Spring Girl flowing through you, bringing life, happiness, wellbeing and freedom and joy.

Relax your arms and enjoy this feeling for a few moments.

(Pause)

When you are ready to finish this meditation:

Take a deep breath. Wiggle your fingers and toes.

Smile at your body and at the world. Open your eyes, stretch.

Summer Girl (Ovulation phase) Meditation

Social restrictions and boundaries can be very challenging for all four Cycle-Girls. But for Summer Girl the lack of touch to show love and caring, the lack of being sociable with friends, and the lack of being around people and doing things in group environments can be particularly difficult. Being with people not only brings joy but it strengthens her emotionally as well.

Your Daughter may not be able to go out to socialise in the way she wants to, but you can give her a little of what she needs in meditation. You can bring her the joy of being with people, creating things together, and the feeling of being touched and of touching. The more emotions you put into reading this meditation, the deeper your Daughter will experience the meditation and meet her needs.

> To help create a balanced ovulation phase, read the Summer Girl Meditation **in the phase**.

A Summer Girl Meditation

Preparation:

You don't need to have anything specific for this meditation, but it's nice to have an image or an object that represents the energies of Summer Girl / the ovulation phase / the Full Moon. Your Daughter may also wish to wear something that expresses her Summer Girl energies.

Meditation

Close your eyes and take a deep breath.

(Pause)

See, know or feel that you stand in front of an ancient tree.

Its branches reach out above you, and its green leaves shelter you from the sun. Birds sing in the tree's branches.

Under your feet, large roots grow in a complex pattern over the earth.

Between two roots is a small spring, and the song of the water fills the air.

Take a deep breath, smile. It feels like home.

(Pause)

At the foot of the tree the Earth Mother sits on a richly embroidered blanket. She wears a simple dress and a wreath of summer flowers.

Two children sit on the tree roots beside her, playing with a ginger and white kitten.

The Earth Mother stands and, smiling, opens her arms to hug you in welcome.

As she holds you, you feel her love surround you – and you relax a little more.

Take a deep breath.

Relax even more.

Let go.

Feel that you are safe.

You rest your head against her, and you know that you are held with love.

(Pause)

The Earth Mother helps you to sit on the rug, and the children place the kitten in your lap.

You stroke its soft fur, feeling its happy purr. Enjoy stroking the cat and feel its contentment flow into your heart and body.

(Pause)

The sound of music announces the arrival of a small group of girls from a nearby village. Laughing and joking, they unpack a picnic, and they call out welcomes to you as they work.

Soon there is a small fire, and the Earth Mother asks if you would like to help. You join the other girls making food. As you chop and mix ingredients your heart opens. You feel that you belong, and that you are one big family.

(Pause)

As the meal cooks and the sun starts to set a few girls begin to play music.

The sparks of the fire rise into the night sky. You are surrounded by beautiful voices singing traditional songs.

You feel relaxed and content. You have a bowl of good food, and the kitten is curled up asleep on your lap. You know that you are surrounded by good friends and you are part of their love.

Relax and enjoy this feeling for as long as you wish.

(Pause)

When you are ready to finish this meditation:

Take a deep breath. Wiggle your fingers and toes.

Smile at your body and at the world. Open your eyes, stretch.

Autumn Girl (Pre-menstrual phase) Meditation

Telling an Autumn Girl what she can or cannot do is never a good idea! Detailed lists of rules and regulations can easily generate feelings of confusion, and of being trapped and powerless – at a time when the Autumn Girl may be vibrating with energy that needs release. These feelings can quickly develop into frustration and then anger, and if there is no 'safe' creative way to release this energy it can spill out into everyday life.

Your Daughter may find it difficult to manage the intense Autumn Girl experiences, but through meditation you can give her the release and magic that she needs to express. You can create the opportunity for her to safely release the anger and shape it into something beautiful and magical. The more Autumn Girl feels the magic in the meditation, the greater her sense of wholeness.

> To create a balanced pre-menstrual phase, read the Autumn Girl Meditation **in the phase.**

An Autumn Girl Meditation

Preparation:

You don't need to have anything specific to undertake this meditation, but it's nice to have an image or an object that represents the energies of the Autumn Girl / pre-menstrual phase / Autumn / decreasing Moon energies. Your Daughter may also wish to wear something to express her Autumn Girl energies.

Meditation

Close your eyes and bring your awareness into your body.

Take a deep breath, and feel that you are standing on a beach with waves crashing against the shore. The low dark clouds of a storm lie above you, and you hold your cloak tightly around you against the strong wind.

You feel the wild power of the storm forcing you to let go and to release the cloak and your tension.

In the wind you hear a female voice calling out, "Let go! Feel the wild energy and be free!"

(Pause)

In the foaming waves in front of you, you see a head above the water – a woman with long black hair and large beautiful eyes of emerald green. A flash of light, and you see the silver scales of a fish-like tail.

She calls to you to join her in the waves – and you cannot resist.

You let the cloak go and the wind whips it away from you.

Suddenly you are in the water, feeling the powerful energy of the waves surrounding you and filling you with wild joy. Like a dolphin you leap over the waves to plunge back into the water.

(Pause)

The energy of the waves vibrates within you as you crash through them, sending spray high into the air. There is no difference between you and the water, and you can feel your waves hitting the rocks.

Experience the joy as the water crashes over the land, breaking down the boundaries that hold you restricted. Again and again your energies crash against the land with wild freedom.

(Pause)

Suddenly the magic of the Merwoman surrounds you, and a gentle hand touches your shoulder. The Merwoman swims close to you, and you see that her skin is covered with soft silver scales and her hair is decorated with small plaits and seashells. A single gemstone radiating light lies on her forehead, held in place by a thin headband made of silver.

Smiling, she takes your hand and gently draws you under the crashing waves into calm. The deeper you go, the calmer the water becomes – and you feel the raging powers soften within you. In the feeling of gentleness, you let go of your inner chaos and feel a softer form of magic.

(Pause)

You land on the seabed into a mystical realm of beauty and light. In wonder, you see the creatures of the sea swimming around you, radiant in their energies and magic. The Merwoman takes an old discarded shell and, wrapping her magic around it, she sings. Beneath her hands the shell becomes carved into the shape of a beautiful seahorse. Another shell becomes a beautiful jewel of the lightest purple colour.

She offers you a shell, and holding it in your hands your palms begin to glow with light. Gently you stroke the shell with your magic and shape it into the design that your heart desires. With delight you feel your hands, heart and magic combine to create.

It feels so good that you take another old shell, and then another. You weave your magic through your hands and create beauty in the world.

Notice the shapes that are woven by your magic.

(Pause)

Enjoy this place of calm and beauty for as long as you wish.

(Pause)

When you are ready to leave this meditation:

Offer your thanks to the Merwoman by giving her one of your creations.

Listen for any advice that you are given.

Take a deep breath. Wiggle your fingers and toes.

Smile at your body and at the world. Open your eyes, stretch.

Winter Girl (Menstrual phase) Meditation

In a stressful situation, women often just 'keep going' through their menstrual phase. They go deep into their emergency reserves of energy to try to motivate themselves. They do things half asleep, and because of the anxiety filling their bodies with stress chemicals they force themselves to be active in the world when their **natural state is to withdraw.**

Winter Girl needs to rest, and she needs her inner focus time to connect to her deepest self so that she can renew her energies and experience her inner wisdom to make heartfelt decisions.

Your Daughter may find it difficult to rest or sleep during a crisis or a demanding situation due to stress and anxiety, but you can help her to experience the deep rest and 'letting go' that she needs, through meditation. You can create the environment for her to release her fear and tension and to once again trust that all will be well. The more Winter Girl lets go in the meditation, the greater her relaxation.

> To create a balanced menstrual phase,
> read the Winter Girl Meditation **in the phase.**

A Winter Girl Meditation

Preparation:

You don't need to have anything specific to undertake this meditation, but it's nice to have an image or an object in front of you that represents the energies of the Winter Girl / menstruation / Winter / Dark Moon energies. Your

Daughter may like to do this meditation lying down – it doesn't matter if she goes to sleep.

Meditation

Close your eyes and bring your awareness into your body.

You sit in a cave with a small fire at the centre. The floor is covered with red and gold rugs, and the space is filled by the warm golden light of the fire.

An old woman wearing a black cloak sits by the fire warming a pot of liquid. Occasionally she adds a few dried herbs. The cave is silent except for the crackling of the fire, and the outside world seems a long way away.

(Pause)

The old woman pulls back her dark hood, and you see her face in the firelight. Dark blue tattoos circle her cheeks, and her dark skin is lined with age. Her thin white hair is caught up in a bun, and her eyes sparkle with welcome and love. She indicates that you should sit by the fire, and she fills a bowl with her tea and hands it to you.

As you sip the tea and taste its comforting flavour, you gaze into the fire's glow and let the flames take away all your thoughts and worries. Some things flow easily and are changed by the flames into light, and you feel relaxation flowing through your body.

You take a deep breath.

(Pause)

Some worries resist the flames – maybe you are fearful that by letting go you will forget them, or that they will no longer be important to you.

The old woman sits next to you, and she places her hand on yours. You feel her love and a deep calm flowing from her to you.

Now the remaining worries flow easily into the flames.

You take another deep breath, and you fill with love. Around you the cave fills with stars and galaxies.

(Pause)

You feel at peace with everything.

You feel acceptance of everything as it is.

You feel hope and healing light flow into your body.

(Pause)

When you are ready to leave this meditation:

Bring your awareness to your heart, and thank the old woman.

Listen for her advice.

Take a deep breath. Wiggle your fingers and toes.

 Smile at your body and at the world. Open your eyes, stretch.

CHAPTER 7
ADVANCED INFORMATION

You now have the basics - but there are a few extra things to consider.

THE BLENDING OF CYCLES

Throughout this book, the Mother's understanding of her own cycle has been treated as an important aspect of understanding and living with her Daughter. The phase of the Mother influences the phase of the Daughter through the Mother's behaviour, and the phase of the Daughter influences the phase of the Mother through the Daughter's behaviour. By understanding your own cycle you are better able to bring wellbeing, balance and happiness to yourself so that you are **stable and empowered** in any of your phases and so more able to manage and process the behaviour and needs of your Daughter's phase.

We have been focusing mainly on your Daughter's cycle, but we also need to consider the interaction between the phases of your own cycle with hers. Here are a few ideas on how the different phase energies can interact with each other.

How your phases can interact with each other

Your Daughter's phase	
	**She is Winter Girl.** She will need rest and quiet. She has little energy or motivation to do anything. Lack of rest or forcing her to do things when she is tired will probably create an irritated and frustrated response. She may be dreamy, able to let go and simply 'be'.

Your phase	
	**You are Dynamic Woman.** You are full of energy and wanting to do things. Perhaps you want to lift her mood and cheer her up. Maybe you are seeing her as a difficult 'moody teenager' who even in a crisis should be more positive and active. *Let her have her quiet time and focus on your own projects and tasks.*
	**You are Loving Woman.** You are empathic and creative; she is withdrawn and hibernating. You want engagement with people, she wants to be left alone. *View giving her space alone when she needs it as an*

	active way to help. Offer quiet and gentle support and be aware that her emotional withdrawal is OK at this time and nothing is wrong.
	**You are Wild Woman.** If you are on a peak of energy, you want things done and fixed, but she is withdrawn and unmotivated. If you have unrealistic expectations of her, you will feel frustrated. If you are in a low energy trough, you may also be withdrawn and feel resentful because she is not helping you. *Keep your expectations of her and of yourself realistic. Do more on your own when you have energy, and give yourself and your Daughter permission to rest when necessary.*
	**You are Wise Woman.** Your energies are low, you lack motivation, but you do have empathy and understanding for her current situation. *Leave chores until another day. You can simply check that she is okay and has everything she needs. Help her to create a sanctuary, or you can curl up together in silence.*

Your Daughter's phase	
	She is Spring Maiden. Her energies are a whirlwind, she has many projects and things she wants to do. She expects you to help when she demands it, otherwise she is doing her own thing independently. Anything she wants or needs has to be done quickly.

Your phase

You are Dynamic Woman.

You have energy, she has energy! You have good thinking skills and so does she. You have a strong ego...and so does she! You will want to work on your projects and meet your goals, and she will want to work on her own goals. This is good – unless one party expects the other party to drop everything to help.

With so much focused achievement, empathy and relationship support may be low priorities on both sides but structure and routine can bring you to together for important interaction.

You are Loving Woman.

She is ego-led, you are love and caring focused. She wants to be independent, and you may want to show love through emotional connection. She is doing lots of things, but she wants to do them alone or with friends, and not with you.

You have the emotional strength to manage but may need some interaction to feel fulfilled. This could be by helping her in some way or creating an activity that she would enjoy – but don't expect more than the minimal interaction!

You are Wild Woman.

If you have an energy peak – she has high energy. If you have a low energy trough – she still has high energy.

With low energy you may be less tolerant of her demands and expectations. You may want to take control of her actions to make her more manageable. You may be more risk-averse if she is trying to be more independent. She needs to know when you have the peaks and troughs – don't expect her to guess.

You are Wise Woman.
You have low energy and are withdrawn. She has increasing energy levels and can be exhausting to be with. You need space to be quiet and rest, she needs space to grow and to explore.
Create routine 'sanctuary breaks' so she knows when you are not available – then you can stay balanced. Try to be structured so that she has the security of knowing what to expect.

Your Daughter's phase

She is Summer Girl.
Her energies are focused towards her friends and helping them. She may also be interested in doing things with the family, and in creative projects. Her physical energies are good, and she can be more open and more emotionally mature and expressive.

Your phase

You are Dynamic Woman.
She has good energies and wants to help; you have increasing energies and want to do your own projects. She wants emotional interaction; you want a list where you can tick off the things you have achieved.
Put 'emotional interaction' with your Daughter on your list! Even if you feel your work tasks and goals are urgent and important, make time to be with her so that she feels part of an interactive loving relationship with you.

You are Loving Woman.
You are emotionally open and caring-focused. She is more emotionally open, and relationship-focused. *Have a heart-to-heart talk, have a family conference for sorting out problems. Both of you will have heightened empathy and good communication and listening skills and will be able to handle problems without negative emotional responses. Win-win!*

You are Wild Woman.
You are decreasing in energy with peaks and troughs and all the associated subconscious stories and emotions. She is stable in energy and in emotions and she needs relationships. She may be more understanding of your frustrations and problems.
In a low, you may feel jealous of the time she shares with her friends and believe your own thoughts telling you that you are not appreciated. But you may find that she is more willing to help with tasks so that you can rest a little more.

You are Wise Woman.
She is empathic and wants to help. You are low in energy and may be more accepting of her help. She can be more understanding and less demanding, but she will still need emotional interaction. She may join you on the sofa to keep you company.
Let her help, delegate tasks to her. Ask her for company when you would like it, but understand that she will look to her friends for her needed emotional interaction.

Your Daughter's phase	
	**She is Autumn Girl.** Her energies are decreasing, with peaks and troughs. She can be highly creative, critical, impulsive and compulsive. She may have many negative stories in her mind, feel overwhelmed, need more sleep. Lack of sleep creates irritability, impatience and frustration.
Your phase	
	**You are Dynamic Woman.** You want to do things, she wants you to do things. You want organisation, she wants destruction! She will be emotional, impulsive, and chaotic but you will need structure, adherence to rules and logic. *Finding a common activity when she has energy can help, but don't expect her energy to last. Try to use some emotional language and empathy.*
	**You are Loving Woman.** You have empathy in this phase for what she is going through. You will want to make things better for her, especially if she is having problems, but she may push you away. *You have the emotional strength and stability to stay with her through any trauma and help her to balance.*
	**You are Wild Woman.** Depending on how you are managing your own phase, you could be reacting to everything she says and does. There could be explosive releases of tension. *Find a quick creative project which you can each do on your own to release energy. Make 'sanctuary time'*

<table>
<tr><td></td><td>when you have time apart from each other to realign and sleep.</td></tr>
<tr><td></td><td>

You are Wise Woman

You will have stability and less connection to the outer world so any tantrums will flow past you. Lack of engagement by you can provoke emotional responses if Autumn Girl does not feel her feelings are validated or that her 'target' for release is not involved.

You can weather the storms, but it is better not to have to. Find a release for her in the peaks and hold her in calm in the troughs.

</td></tr>
</table>

MORE THAN ONE MENSTRUAL DAUGHTER?

Many women think that Mothers and Daughters tend to have their cycles in synch with each other, and that sisters and close friends may also have their cycles synchronised. But there are other women who know that their cycles have never been in synch with their Daughters' or friends' or works colleagues' cycles. Some women do experience synchronised cycles, especially if they have a common view on life or a common perception and purpose, but it is certainly not something that all women experience. Mothers and Daughters and sisters often have very different outlooks on life, different expectations and different goals and life purpose. So, what happens if you are a Mother with two Daughters with different menstrual cycles living closely together? Life gets even more interesting!

The dance of the cycles becomes a pattern of phases that are sometimes in alignment, sometimes in total opposition and sometimes phases that are next to each other in the cycle. The need for self-awareness, self-identification and expression and communication all become even more important to allow a harmonious balancing of energies, needs and motivations. It is important that each phase is validated, similarities and differences acknowledged, and activities that can be done alone or with others identified for specific phases.

Looking at the cycle, it's clear that there is commonality between different pairs of phases:

- Spring Girl and Summer Girl both have good physical energy and are focused on the other world.

- Autumn Girl and Winter Girl both share times of low physical energy and the need for more rest and sleep.

- Spring Girl and Autumn Girl are both phases of changing energy – increasing for the Spring Girl and decreasing for the Autumn Girl. There is a dynamic energy and a focus on the ego that links them.

- Summer Girl and Winter Girl both have stable energy.
  Summer Girl has stable outward-focused energy and Winter Girl has inward-focused energy.

- Spring Girl and Summer Girl can be confident in the world, active in doing things and able to manage people and everyday tasks.

- Autumn Girl and Winter Girl can both be withdrawn and focused inwards, and find words and logic difficult but creative and inspired thinking easy. They may also both be attracted by spirituality.

When you start to observe the different phases of your Daughters you may find strong similarities between phases, which enables you to find a compromise language, an activity, a motivation or a need-fulfilment which will support two different phases at the same time. This is advanced work! But if you get your Daughters involved in the exploration – especially in their Spring Girl phases – they will probably be able to discover ways that they can fulfil each other's needs without you being involved.

So, a family making supper could have Summer Girl helping with the cooking, and Winter Girl finding the cutlery etc. And if you have Spring Girl as well you could ask her to find all the ingredients you need, help with preparation, and ensure that everyone follows the recipe. Summer Girl and Spring Girl would help with washing up afterwards because they know that when they are menstrual it will be their turn to rest.

If you give each Daughter a role or task that they find easy due to their phase then things are more likely to be done quickly and efficiently – and hopefully with minimal resistance.

Finding the win-win solution does require mutual respect, recognition and understanding.

WATCH YOUR LANGUAGE!

Your communication ability and approach can be influenced by your phase, so you need to be aware of the impact of the way you communicate on your Daughter (and your family!).

If you are a Dynamic Woman you are more likely to give your Daughter lots of things to do, and the way you present tasks will be efficient and logical – but it can be perceived as making dictatorial demands. You are also less likely to praise your Daughter for finishing a task, because you are already looking at the next thing on your mental list. This can be interpreted as a lack of appreciation or validation of helping you. Also, with so many things happening – you can be a mega multi-tasker in this phase – you may find it difficult to give your full attention to your Daughter when she is telling you things, which can lead to the accusation that 'You never listen to me!'

In your Loving Woman phase you may want to give more time to your Daughter than to your work. You may find your Daughter opening up to you more because you have better listening skills and you can be less likely to judge or criticise. This naturally creates a safe space for her to approach you with things that she may be worried about. In this phase you may feel a very deep loving connection with your Daughter.

If you are a Wild Woman, then it is important to notice how you communicate when you are not meeting your needs. You may find that you are more likely to be unintentionally very direct, or to snap or to use a negative tone of voice. This is because the subconscious mind thinks more quickly than the conscious mind, and you speak before you think. You are also more likely to come across as judgemental and critical.

The problem is that seeing what is wrong is very easy in this phase, and the obvious way to fix it is to tell someone that they are doing something wrong and explain what they should be doing to make it better. Unfortunately, not everyone sees the Wild Woman's superpower and approach as helpful, and it can be quite hurtful to be on the receiving end. Where possible, try to focus your superpower somewhere else to release it so that it doesn't come into your communications.

Also be aware that in this phase your mind is highly creative, and it is looking for possible negative situations as a defence mechanism – if you can think of a negative situation then you can prepare for it in advance. However, this tendency may create an avalanche of negative scenarios… 'if she goes to the supermarket to get milk, she could catch a virus and then she would be ill, and the rest of the family could get it from a door handle and my elderly parents could die of it, or my Daughter could die or I could die and leave the family without a mother and their lives would be destroyed!'

It's important to catch the creative thought process at 'if she goes to the supermarket to get milk, she could catch a virus,' and then make preparations to keep her safe while she is away from the home environment. Projecting all the negative scenarios WITH the emotional reactions that you are feeling as you think about them is not fair on your Daughter or your family. But it can be hard to prevent this avalanche of thoughts, so just be aware that:

1. the thoughts are not true

2. the thoughts are part of a fully functioning alert system

3. your dominant subconscious is using its creativity to help you to prepare for a situation and to clear away any old emotional baggage from the subconscious that is attached to it. This is why women need some space in their Wild Woman phase – they need time alone to process the thoughts and emotions so that they don't share them with others when it's not necessary.

OTHER INFLUENCES ON WOMEN'S CYCLES

There can also be many other influences impacting on your Daughter's experiences of the Cycle-Girls:

- Lack of sleep.

- Anxiety and fear.

- Working to a tight deadline: homework / revision.

- Multi-tasking expectations: schoolwork / social life / hobbies.

- Overwhelming stressful circumstances: exams / change of class or school / parent relationship break-up / divorce / bereavement / new family / new home / changes in routine / changes in life.

- Life decision stress: choosing school subjects / boyfriend or girlfriend relationships / growing sexual awareness.

- Anticipation.

- High ambition.

- Medication.

- Falling in love / breaking up.

- Bullying / relationship issues.

- Identity issues.

- Contraceptive medication.

Every woman is unique, and you have an amazing opportunity to truly discover the amazing young woman who is growing in your life. Don't limit your understanding of who she is because you don't want to have to adapt — instead, simply be aware of her changes and of the things that might be influencing her in addition to her cycle.

HELPING YOUR DAUGHTER TO GROW IN AWARENESS OF HER CYCLIC NATURE

If you want to help your older Daughter to explore further her cyclic energies, she may like to read some of my other books:

Dynamic Woman phase reading:
'The Optimized Woman – Using your menstrual cycle to create success and fulfilment'

Loving Woman phase reading:
'Female Energy Awakening – The path of the Worldwide Womb Blessing back to Authentic Femininity'

Wild Woman phase reading:
'Red Moon – Understanding and using the creative, sexual and spiritual gifts of the menstrual cycle'

Wise Woman phase reading:
'Spiritual Messages for Women – Feminine wisdom for the menstrual cycle'

A NOTE FOR PERI-MENOPAUSE AND POST-MENOPAUSE MOTHERS

Peri-menopause

Peri-menopause is the time before your last menstruation when your hormone levels start to change and your cycles begin to become more erratic. Welcome to your

Daughter's world! You are going through a second stage of adolescence – but instead of growing into a fertile adult woman, you are growing into the ultimate stage of human female development!

Like your Daughter you are changing. Like your Daughter you are not growing 'old', instead you are 'growing up'.

During peri-menopause, your cycles start to become irregular, with some phases lasting months and other lasting just a few days. You may even experience all four phases in a single day! As your menstrual periods grow further apart, you are no longer able to predict from your diary which phase you are going to be in, so now you have to listen to your body and become an explorer to discover who you are on any single day. Then you can create well-being by meeting your needs and expressing your enhanced abilities and energies as and when they appear.

If you understand your cycle then, like your Daughter, you can create a sailing boat and navigate through the high waves and storms. Like your Daughter, you can understand the challenges of not knowing who you are or what you are like with any predictability. Like your Daughter, some days you will manage your inner changes and the outer changes in the world, and on other days everything will feel too much for you. You are both in a state of flux – but this doesn't mean that you can't create balance within yourself or within your relationship with your Daughter. In fact, you have more in common with her – because you are both going through a life-changing experience. At the end of the change you will feel comfortable with who you are and she will be comfortable with who she is, and the journey you have taken together will have created a deep and lasting bond.

Post-menopause

The word 'menopause' is the term used for your final bleeding, so 'menopause' only lasts for a few days! However, menopause is not the end of your changes – it is actually the middle of your changes. Peri-menopause can start around the age of 40 or even earlier, menopause can occur around the age of 50, and based on women's experiences it seems that the physical, perceptual and energy changes can continue for at least a further 10 years. This is your Wild Woman stage of life. But don't despair! The further you leave menopause behind, the more stable your energies become, the more solid your sense of your new non-cyclic self, and the more you enter the Wise Woman stage of your life.

Just like women in peri-menopause, you need to observe who you are and meet the need for expression of your energies as they arise. If you have not been able to observe your own cycle experiences during your fertile adult years, you can use your observations of your Daughter's phases to help you to identify which of the four Cycle-Women you are currently expressing. **The joy comes when you feel a sense of centredness within yourself and can recognise and use the gifts of the cycle without needing a cycle to give you access to them.**

Many women who are post-menopause still like to live a practical cyclic life. Some women feel connected to the cycle of the Moon, and alter their activities to fit the lunar cycle:

Dynamic Woman phase – 3 days after the Dark Moon ('New Moon') to 3 days before the Full Moon.

Loving Woman phase – 3 days before the Full Moon to 3 days after the Full Moon.

Wild Woman phase – 3 days after the Full Moon to 3 days before the Dark Moon ('New Moon')

Wise Woman phase – 3 days before the Dark Moon ('New Moon') to 3 days after the Dark Moon.

Other women feel more connected to the Earth and her cycles, so they match their activities to the energies of the season:

Dynamic Woman phase – Spring months.

Loving Woman phase – Summer months.

Wild Woman phase – Autumn months.

Wise Woman phase – Winter months.

Living in this way can help you keep an awareness of the cyclic nature of your Daughter as she grows into adulthood and enable you to empathise with her experiences, even if you had your menopause several years ago.

CHAPTER 8
AND FINALLY...

We women are on a journey of cycle discovery. For each of us, this journey lasts for the length of our cyclic life – but the benefits for the relationship between Mothers and Daughters have the potential to last a lifetime. Cycle awareness breaks down the barriers between generations; it gives all women something in common whether they are young women just starting their cyclic life, women with many years' experience of their cycle, or women who have moved beyond the cycle but can look back with knowledge and wisdom.

The Cycle also helps us to understand each other's generation, because in every month we journey between life stages and experiences – whatever our age we are a young woman again in the pre-ovulation phase, we know what it is like to be a mother in the ovulation phase, we experience the creative energy of the peri-menopause and early post-menopause woman, and then we know what it is like to be the slow, old mystical woman at menstruation. There is no division between the ages for women – we are all these ages within our cycle, so we have the benefits and gifts available to us at any age and we are prepared for the future because we know what we are going to be like.

But most importantly, without age barriers limiting our perception we empathise with other women and can recognise our commonality. Mothers and Daughters share all stages of womanhood. Daughters also share her womanhood with her sisters, aunts, female cousins, and grandmothers. With this understanding, our behaviour can change towards each other and we can support women in an appropriate way when things are challenging, and we can understand and forgive when overwhelm makes behaviour excessive.

We women *are* complex, but it is this complexity that gives us such amazing gifts, skills and abilities, creativity and insight. For too long our complexity has been seen as too difficult to manage, and so we have been forced into a man-shaped box to make things easier for everyone. We have achieved amazing things – we have gone into space, won Nobel Peace Prizes, led countries, led multi-national companies, been celebrities, doctors, healthcare workers, pilots, farmers, industry leaders, entrepreneurs, lawyers, accountants, managers, teachers, scientists, spiritual leaders – the world is a different place because we women have been changing it. But everything we have achieved has been with restrictions and limitations on who we are and what we can do when. Imagine what your Daughter's generation will achieve if they are released and have the freedom to fully express who they are when they are!

What starts as a way to try to live together in better harmony has the potential to develop into a new way of women understanding themselves, working together and of changing the world to make it more accessible to women. It's not going to happen by fighting men, it's going to happen by one Mother sharing her cycle and experiences with her Daughter and showing how amazing the gifts can be.

Worldwide insecurity, financial meltdowns, global pandemics, pending environmental catastrophe, civil unrest, increasing international isolation, and rapidly changing technology, social relations and regulations can all create anxiety and stress – but they can also offer a wonderful opportunity for Mothers and Daughters to:

- become closer

- explore and understand each other's cyclic nature

- live a more practical everyday cyclic life

- build more mutual respect

- support each other in appropriate ways

- forgive and forget when the situation overwhelms the phase

- build a deeper relationship of shared feminine understanding

- discover how empowering it can be when women live and work together in awareness and acceptance for their different phases.

Women adapt to living and working against their cyclic nature because the world still doesn't recognise or accept their natural cycles as a powerful and positive influence and a resource of valuable skills and abilities. But the more we learn about living and working together with our cycles the more difficult it will be to fit in with these old outdated expectations and assumptions of who we are.

We can't go back – we can't lose what we have learned by living through challenging global and personal changes. We have to bring our cyclic nature into our life and work in small ways so that we can keep the benefits we have discovered through adversity. And if we do that, we continue to be role models of cycle awareness for our Daughters – and perhaps their generation will break down the barriers and ignorance and prejudice further and there will be a society that values, encourages and sees the benefit of women's cyclic nature.

A SUMMARY

A few things to remember:

❖ There are things you will share in common with your Daughter, and things that she will experience in a different way.

❖ Try not to make the mistake of thinking that your experience is the only valid one and that what works for you should work for her.

❖ Your role is to create the space to let her discover who she is and how she relates to the world.

❖ She is four different Cycle-Girls in one body, and she expresses each girl in alignment with a particular menstrual cycle phase.

❖ If you have a cycle, you too have four Cycle-Women within you, and how you interact with your Daughter will depend on which woman you are currently experiencing.

❖ Each Cycle-Girl has her own physical energy levels, dominant thinking, enhanced abilities and skills, and motivation and needs.

❖ Actively living daily life recognising the phase that your Daughter is experiencing can reduce her stress, increase happiness and wellbeing, and help to create a harmonious balance within the family.

❖ Your Daughter will learn from you, so know your cycle and be a role model of living your life supporting your cyclic needs and expressing your enhanced skills and motivations.

❖ Doing a task which fulfils a phase need or expresses a phase-enhanced ability, within the phase, creates feelings of wellbeing and happiness.

❖ Where possible, avoid tasks that don't fit phase abilities or energies, adapt them, or adjust your expectations of how long they will take or how easy they will be to do.

❖ Recognise that the world doesn't allow women to live a 100% cyclic life – so do the best you can under the circumstances.

❖ Notice the way you are communicating with your Daughter – are you matching her phase thinking? Are you instead expressing your phase thinking and ignoring hers?

❖ It seems a lot to observe and think about at first, but together you will create a shorthand language where you can quickly express who you are and what you want or need to do.

- ❖ There are no 'right' or 'wrong' activities or approaches – there are only ones that fit better with a specific phase.

- ❖ Sometimes life will overwhelm your phase – this is OK.

- ❖ If there are issues, wait a few days for the phase to change, and then try again.

- ❖ If you have had a challenging month, you have an opportunity to try something new in the next month.

- ❖ Remember that this is a path of learning and of moving forwards and growing together. You can never go backwards – this is a spiralling path. Every phase in every month will be unique because of changing circumstances, but this makes the journey exciting as you and your Daughter have the opportunity in every month to grow as women.

- ❖ Don't give up! Check your phase – meet your needs – try something different.

- ❖ Make notes – this is because we often find it difficult to remember what we are like in a phase unless we are experiencing the phase – especially in the menstrual phase.

❖ Look for the positives within each phase (of both your own cycle and your Daughter's cycle) and you will discover the gifts.

❖ Everyone has their own experiences – this book works with generalisations. It is up to you to know your cyclic Daughter.

It's not easy being cyclic in a linear masculine world. It's not easy being cyclic with global changes and societal anxieties, demands, restrictions and regulations. We can't expect the attitude towards women to change overnight, but we can make small changes in our lives to bring happiness and wellbeing – and then when the world creates its new 'normal' we can take our knowledge and experience out into the world and change that 'normal' for the better. It will be your Daughter's generation – inspired by your generation – that will make sure that the cyclic nature of women becomes respected as a positive force for society and for work.

Observe
Try
Adapt
Try again

Appendix

A TEACHING STORY

This story is a fun way to introduce the menstrual cycle to younger girls, and it comes from my book '*Female Energy Awakening*' where a sequence of First Woman stories help women to understand their menstrual cycle wisdom in a more creative and imaginative approach.

The Making of the World

At the making of the world, First Woman opened her eyes and looked around at the trees and the sky, at the river and the mountains, and she asked the first words: 'Who am I?'

And the First Animals of the world responded, and they came to tell her. Hare Woman came forward and gave First Woman a flower.

'You are Hare,' she said.

Then Horse Woman left her herd and gave First Woman a mirror.

'You are Horse,' she said.

Owl Woman swooped in, dropping a curved knife at First Woman's feet.

'You are Owl,' she cried.

And Bear Woman sat in front of First Woman and gave her an obsidian bowl.

'You are Bear,' she growled.

First Woman looked at the animals, puzzled, and asked: 'But how can I be all of you?'

So Serpent Woman came up to First Woman and placed a belt around her hips. She attached each object to the belt.

'You are Serpent.' she said. 'You flow'.

Moon Mother suddenly appeared, bathing them all in her beauty and light.

'Ah, First Daughter, you have discovered who you are,' she said, smiling.

First Woman looked at her belt, then looked up at Moon Mother.

'But how will I know when I am Hare Clan, Horse Clan, Owl Clan or Bear Clan?' she asked.

Moon Mother replied 'I will show you from the sky.

Watch my face grow and be with the Hare people, see my full smile and be with Horse clan, see my face incline and be with the Owl people and then, when I leave the sky, follow me and hibernate with the Bear Clan'.

And First Woman knew who she was.

WHERE DOES THIS INFORMATION COME FROM?

About the author

Miranda Gray is an international author and women's workshop teacher. Her first book on the menstrual cycle 'Red Moon: Understanding and using the creative, sexual and spiritual gifts of the menstrual cycle' was first published in 1994, and since then she has been writing and teaching women around the world about their cyclic nature and how to live this nature practically in a masculine world. Miranda lives in the UK.

Inspired by the 2020 world pandemic crisis and the associated restrictions and social distancing, Miranda felt there was an urgent need for a general and practical guide to help Mothers who may be living in close proximity with their teenaged Daughters under stressful circumstances. This book aims to help Mothers to learn about the phases of their Daughters' cycles and to offer useful ideas and concepts to help them to create a positive, strong, harmonious, and mutually supportive relationship whenever times are challenging.

Miranda hopes that this book will not only help Mothers and Daughters to creatively manage stress and restrictions in a way that is co-supportive, but that they will also learn more about each other and create deeper bonds of love, friendship and understanding which they can take out into the world to create a positive and developing relationship that will last for the rest of their lives.

www.mirandagray.co.uk

FB: mirandagrayhome

Instagram: @mirandagray.author

ALSO BY MIRANDA GRAY

The Optimized Woman: Using your menstrual cycle to achieve success and fulfilment.

If you want to get ahead, get a cycle!
For women who want to create life-success in a female way.

This book is for the 21st-century woman who wants to create wellbeing, fulfilment, work success, goal-achievement and the life she wants using a uniquely female approach.

Miranda Gray answers the question 'What use is my menstrual cycle?' by returning the cycle to its rightful place as a powerhouse of practical resources for women. The little-recognised secret lies in Optimum Times, days of enhanced abilities.

The book offers you a daily plan of Optimum Time practical activities that you can tailor to your circumstances and cycle – whether natural or medically managed. It helps you to identify and achieve your goals, increase excellence, build better relationships, create the ideal work/life balance, and generate personal happiness.

Red Moon: Understanding and using the creative, sexual and spiritual gifts of the menstrual cycle

'The Optimized Woman' offers women a very practical approach to applying the enhanced skills and abilities contained in their menstrual cycles to everyday life, but 'Red Moon' goes deeper into the mystery of women's cyclic nature.

Exploring the ancient female teaching that is still available in mythology and nursery tales, Miranda Gray creates profound understanding of the cycle as a gift that empowers women to renew themselves each month, to manifest and create the world around them, to connect deeply with the land and their family, and to express deep wisdom and inspiration.

Miranda guides modern women through four ancient Female Archetypes to help them to embrace a passionate and creative cycle-empowered life. She explores the women's wisdom contained in Western mythology and traditional stories and offers practical exercises and methods (including the 'Moon Dial') to explore the depths of being a Cyclic Woman.

Female Energy Awakening: The path of the Worldwide Womb Blessing back to Authentic Femininity

Do you desire to live fully as the passionate, spiritual, empowered, loving, creative and sensual woman, you know you truly are?

Five times a year, thousands of women worldwide connect with each other. They connect to walk a path of female healing and a return to their long-forgotten authentic femininity through the **Worldwide Womb Blessing – a Female Energy Awakening**.

In this book, originator Miranda Gray shares the story behind the Worldwide Womb Blessing® and provides new answers to fundamental questions for the modern woman

- Why the womb energy centre is critical to the well-being and happiness of all women, whatever their age or physical condition.

- How the Sacred Feminine is relevant to modern women, and how reconnecting to this principle can lead you to a less stressful life.

- How to fully embrace your femininity in a masculine-centred world that constantly disconnects women from what it means to be truly female.

The included 28-day Womb Blessing Path of Female Conscious Living is an essential guide to your true nature and helps support the healing and awakening that occurs through the Womb Blessing.

Spiritual Messages for Women: Feminine wisdom for the menstrual cycle.

A book that returns to us the secret of living a female spiritual life in a masculine world.

Does your heart cry out for a daily spiritual relationship with the Divine, but it just seems so difficult to hold on to? **There is a secret female-only spiritual path.**

Women's natural spirituality differs from men's spirituality, and yet we expect it to be the same. The key to our perception of and relationship with the Divine is our menstrual cycle. The Divine means different things to us in each phase of our menstrual cycle, and our relationship to Her, our spiritual needs and our spiritual expression change with each phase.

Spiritual Messages for Women offers daily inspirational, supportive and loving guidance in tune with your four cycle phases, showing you how to create and enjoy a wonderful loving relationship with the Divine every day throughout the whole month.

Dip into the sections once a day or throughout the day to reach out to the Divine and join Her dance.

9 798652 519131